Cont

DEDICATION

I dedicate this book first to my mother who has been my best friend, who has been my confidant, my pastor, my counselor and my inspiration for writing this book. For many years I nagged her to write a book about her life not realizing that God had given me the passion to write it myself. "Mom, your life has changed the legacy of our family, the generations to come and will mark the lives of many families around the world."

I dedicate this book to my wonderful and supportive husband, Jay Cotto, alongside our two beautiful girls, Jeseny and Jaylinn. They have supportive me through this journey, listened to me tell the story repeatedly, and most importantly provided a shoulder for my countless tears while writing this book. They provided guidance and a different point of view when I couldn't see outside the story. My husband took care of me while I devoted countless hours writing. My girls inspire me every day to make them proud and become their hero. My oldest daughter, Jeseny, helped me with social media, promoting the book and kept me with a smile when I thought this was too hard for me to do.

I dedicate this book to my immediate family. I pray that we completely heal and overcome whatever life throws at us so we can become who God has created us to be. I pray we don't fear life but embrace it and take risk to reach our dreams and goals. I pray we wake up from our daily routines to realize our dreams were placed in our hearts by God and we must step out in faith and make them happen. I pray we can be united more than ever before to break all those generational curses to change the legacy of our families in our own individual families. A special thanks for my big sister, Janna, who called me every day to see how I was doing with the book and all the emotions that followed suit and Giara, her daughter, who helped with editing the book and making it more passionate.

I dedicate this book to families that are forgotten who at one time where in a position of power. Many families who are in a position of power suffer in silence for years. They live their lives strapped in their own emotions. They are never able to express who they really are because of the image they have to portrait in public. They become addicted to substances to run away for their reality. This book is written for you. There is a way out, hold on and read on.

Finally, I dedicate this book to pastors (leaders) kids and spouses. I see so many of these families in pain, broken, divided and disoriented. So many of them are forgotten. I encourage you to press through, forgive, let go and move on. Be who you were created to be. It's not over yet if you're reading this book. Prevail and embrace the process of overcoming.

Thank You

There Are Concepts That Are Sometimes Difficult To Express…

I am extremely blessed to have a mother appointed by God who has shaped my life. I know that many women do not have this blessing, but whether it's through blood or not, God always places someone in our path to guide us.

Although many women see their mothers differently, each one contributes to the next generation. When a woman becomes a mother, she becomes the center of her child's world. She becomes their everything, from their eyes, arms, and feet, to an affectionate hug. Step by step, they help develop us inside out until we are mature enough to stand on our own. A mother always goes beyond imagination and expectations. Whatever happens, they will always be there for us.

Many consider "MOTHERHOOD" a synonym to love, nurturing, devotion, and sacrifice, amongst many other things. When in reality, "Motherhood" goes so much deeper than that. A mother can have secrets. A mother can have hopes and dreams. A mother can go through silent battles. A mother can stand in the gap of her children's short comings. But the one thing I am sure of, is that LOVE with stands it all.

Mommy,

God bless you for the love you've instilled in me.

God bless you for the joy and peace in your heart.

God bless you for your virtue and integrity.

God bless you for your silence, but above all

God bless you for shaping me as your daughter.

Many women cannot stand the ups and downs of life. Some try to sustain themselves by pride, others by submission, but mine by love.

I hope this will awaken something inside you that you did not know existed. As you read on, I know God will begin an inner healing in you that will take you to a place of confrontation and alinement to sustain your freedom for which you were created.

My mother remained standing in every storm of her life. She lived through religious and domestic abuse by my father's hands. She grew up with the principle of "do not say anything; nobody has to know; this stays in the family." She lived behind a mask of submission which led her to a place of guilt. She learned to live with inner pain for the sake of her children.

For generations, many women and men have experienced various types of abuse: religious, social, physical, verbal, psychological, etc. I'll discuss each in this book but, I'll focus on one thing that has to be addressed and eliminated: Religious abuse.

For a long time, I thought about writing this book but, I didn't feel the opportune moment until now. The goal of this book is not to judge or belittle anyone, but to honor my mother's sacrifices and inner strength while, promoting inner healing to those that have been victims in their own homes. It's to enlighten you—not to kill your seed, but to let it sprout into your destiny.

Every man and women should know that someone out there has survived multiple types of abuse and has lived on successfully through God's healing. We need to understand that many families in power and in the public eye, are actually being victimized in private. It's time to open the curtains and see what's been behind. What you see and admire, is not always true behind closed doors.

I hope that by reading this book you will learn skills that will help you overcome your situation. My desire is that you will become free and live the life the Creator, My God, had in mind for you when you were forming in the womb of your mother. May this book give you hope.

Today is the day you'll receive answers to all your unanswered questions. How long will this go on? How long do I have to endure this pain? Why am I going through this and for what?

The narcissist believe they are always right. They want all the accolades and rewards. They are attention seekers who nurture their self-image of greatness. They firmly believe that everyone exists to serve their wants and needs. Whoever chooses otherwise is a threat to who they are, and they will try to destroy them or alienate them from there circle. This is what I saw and lived behind closed doors in my own home. The narcissist leader believes they are a good leader but, they are really a destructive one.

Religious abuse is real, and it has yet to be uncovered.

Mommy, your silence shaped my life. I want you to always believe in your heart, that I am capable of confronting life because of what I saw, what I've lived through and above all, everything you've given me.

INTRODUCTION

You're going to read about two women who grew up in two different generations but share a bond in their similar stories. You'll see how generational curses exist and how you can break them if you're willing to identify them, demask them, confront them and change them into blessings. Some parts are funny, some parts are painful, but each part will bring you to prevail in your storms. I speak the truth. The truth allows you to prevail.

I Identify all the lies you've been told and help you leave them behind to move forward with your life. The truth will always set you free. It's time to stop the guilt and shame we feel when breaking the cycle of abuse and narcissism. Stop thinking about what others think about and decide to be free. Decide to feel peace and joy. The process of overcoming will allow you to enjoy the journey and embrace true freedom.

You will stop feeling that you're not good enough and start believing that you were created for greatness.

You will respect yourself with nothing else but greatness!

That's why I'm writing this book. That's why I do what I do. That's why I love to talk to men and women about their greatness. That's why I pray that your life will change when you read this book!

My mother lived a life of abuse for over 33 years. I personally experienced her struggle and how she overcame those inner battles to become the women God has created to be. She figured out how to live a life of joy through the abuse she experienced. We all have something we need to overcome in life, but not all do. Many take that abuse or struggle to their grave and never see what's on the other side of their darkness.

The goal of this book is for us to know without a shadow of a doubt that you can conquer whatever life throws at you. Did my mother know that at 4 years old she would suffer a trauma that literally would shape her life? Although she found herself in trauma and in a cycle of all types of abuse, there was something inside of her that allowed her to reach out to the almighty God to understand that there was a higher purpose why she went through that pain and suffering. Did she understand that while she was going through it? No. But while she was suffering, the peace of God that surpasses all understanding carried her through it.

A lot of us question, Why? Why me? What did I do? Was it my fault? When is joy going to come? So many questions my mother asked herself while in the mist of her abuse. But the love she had for us as a mother propelled her to survive through the times when she thought she was drowning in pain.

In the same way, the peace of God propelled me through my story. I will share dark times, troubling times, traumatic times, scandalous times, unforgettable times and joyful times about my life as well. You'll see that if you don't put a stop to generational curses, you and your future generations will have to endure the same cycle.

I remember through that pain and trauma, there was a reminder by God telling my mother, "Don't forget who you are. You are a virtuous woman." The Bible in Proverbs 31 talks about an epilogue of the NOBLE WIFE. I can't describe my mother any clearer than this.

Proverbs 31:10,12-22, 24-31 New International Version (NIV)

Epilogue: The Wife of Noble Character

[10] [a] A wife of noble character who can find? She is worth far more than rubies.[12] She brings him good, not harm, all the days of her life.[13] She selects wool and flax and works with eager hands. [14] She is like the merchant ships, bringing her food from afar.[15] She gets up while it is still night; she provides food for her family and portions for her female servants.[16] She considers a field and buys it; out of her earnings she plants a vineyard.[17] She sets about her work vigorously; her arms are strong for her tasks.[18] She sees that her trading is profitable, and her lamp does not go out at night.[19] In her hand she holds the distaff and grasps the spindle with her fingers.[20] She opens her arms to the poor and extends her hands to the needy.[21] When it snows, she has no fear for her household; for all of them are clothed in scarlet.[22] She makes coverings for her bed; she is clothed in fine linen and purple.[24] She makes linen garments and sells them, and supplies the merchants with sashes.[25] She is clothed with strength and dignity; she can laugh at the days to come. [26] She speaks with wisdom, and faithful instruction is on her tongue. [27] She watches over the affairs of her household and does not eat the bread of idleness.[28] Her children arise and call her blessed; her husband also, and he praises her:[29] "Many women do noble things, but you surpass them all."[30] Charm is deceptive, and beauty is fleeting; but a woman who fears the LORD is to be praised.*[31] Honor her for all that her hands have done, and let her works bring her praise at the city gate.*

I was about 16-17 years old at the time when I remember there was a contest in the association of churches, we participated in to celebrate a woman the congregation felt had the characteristics of a virtuous woman. Although the women of the church wanted to enter my mother in the contest, no one did. Everyone forgot. Once the day came to choose the virtuous woman, somehow, some way, miraculously my mother's name came out of the hat. It wasn't a miracle, it was destiny. God was reminding her, although you are going through the valley of the shadow of death, in My eyes you are virtuous. I remember like it was yesterday how she was celebrated. I was so proud of her, especially that she was my mommy and I would go home with her.

Through your pain, God will always remind you who you are in His eyes. Someone special. Someone unique. Someone powerful who can achieve the dreams and goals God has placed in your heart. Someone with an unstoppable destiny. Someone chosen for greatness. Our process is to identify what that greatness is and stop trying to escape your process. This is your season, your hour, your time, to walk into your destiny. You are not defined by what has happened to you.

You are going to read some disturbing stories but keep reading to see the victory at the end. God will never give you pain without giving you an escape from it. He will provide peace, joy and freedom through your struggle. Don't get weary in well doing, the Bible says, and it will pay great dividends.

THIS IS THE STORY...

Chapter 1

HELPLESS

The Beginning Does Not Define the END…

Before I begin to explain the steps of inner healing caused by abuse, I want to share a bit of history of the life of my mother, Lumi.

She was born in the city of Ponce on the island of Puerto Rico. She the youngest of two girls. She was shy and introverted, but a series of events changed who she was. She went from trials and struggles to victory and triumph.

Here goes her story…

Her relationship with her grandparents was beautiful. She loved being with them. She remembers running through the fields, enjoying nature and being nurtured and loved by them. It seemed like a normal family unit. Unfortunately, at the age of 4 she experienced an extremely traumatic and painful event. As she left her grandparents room to go play outside, she heard a loud noise and a scream. She saw her mother run into the room and when she looked inside, she saw her grandfather gasping for air. Not understanding exactly what was happening, she saw her mother dragging a 6-foot-tall man out the house to get him medical help. She heard her mother scream, "Why did you do this? Why are you trying to take your life?" She looked at her grandfather as he tried to talk to her mother but, instead she saw him take his last breath. She later discovered he committed suicide to escape the dreadful news that her grandmother was terminally ill and was given days to live.

This, without knowing it, shaped her life. Leading her to desperately seek the love and nurturing she lost from her grandparents.

The department of education states that the first five years of a child's life are especially crucial for physical, intellectual and social-emotional development. I believe this tragic event had a lot to do with why she coped with extreme abuse later in her years.

"I will never forget that event"

I remember her saying, "I will never forget that event."

Here is some information that's crucial in a child's development. "Trauma in children's developmental years are more common than we would like to accept. A series of studies done by psychologists of Duke University Medical School, reveals that 78% of children have reported to experience one to various traumatic experiences before the age of 5 years old. At 6 years old, 20% have experienced sexual abuse, emotional neglect, domestic violence, and/or a tragic loss." With this, I must agree that the enemy (devil) is always trying to attack our children, to destroy their dreams and goals. Their overall destiny. The Great Book,

The Bible, states in John 10:10, "The thief (devil) comes only to steal, kill and destroy…

She describes her childhood thereafter being sad and lonely. Her dad was always sick; he came back physical and mentally ill from the Korean War. Nothing was the same. His stories were extremely gruesome and horrible to discuss. Her mother had to work out of necessity to financially support the family. Her father had his own money. He would give a portion to her mother to take care of her and her sister, Elsie, but it wasn't enough. She was alone a lot with her sister. She was not even ten years old yet and she vividly remembers standing inside their home where she could hear her parents arguing outside.

"I don't want to work anymore," her mother was saying. "Give me more money so I can buy meat and food for the girls."

Her father was no longer there. Instead stood an old, bitter man who seemed to have something against his young wife. He was twenty years older than her mother when they married. Her mother was around 25 years old, and very much still beautiful and spunky as ever. She spent all her days and nights away bringing home all she could before getting back to the grind. It seemed the more time she spent away, the more she found other places, and other people to spend her time with. The farther and farther apart they became. Although her father came back sick from the war, he didn't seem to care about the well-being of the family.

"No," he told her flatly. And that was that. Her mother had to continue working and Lumi had to grow up without her.

Lumi knew something wasn't right. She knew her mother was getting what she needed from someone else. But it was one thing to know and another to see.

She knew her mother wanted the best for them but, that life-style created an emptiness and sadness in her heart. Lumi, had to raise herself. She would stay up at night to watch her father sleep, afraid he would choke at night due to his breathing issues. She learned to cook and clean on her own. On the contrary as she reserved her persona; her sister, Elsie, was extremely social and extraverted. She, being the youngest, was easily dominated and bullied by her sister. Elsie didn't allow her to go the parties with her or socialize with her. She was the queen bee in every event and number one in all the sports and contest she participated in. While it appeared Lumi was just timid; in reality, her insecurities were being birthed.

Think about this: when we are born, we come completely "helpless." We have the need for food, heat, clothing, sleep, etc... However, if in the process of our parents obtaining these things, our socio-emotional needs are not met, then trauma is created. Children need that physical and verbal attention that helps them build security and affection. Lumi grew up not knowing how to distinguish a secure relationship versus an insecure relationship. She didn't know how to separate who was good for her or who was a danger in her life. She didn't develop defenses of protection and/or limits on who she was going to let enter or refuse in her life.

Lumi did her best not to stay far behind Elsie. She played basketball, ran track and was a cheer leader. When she entered high school, she joined the Reserve Officers' Training Corps (ROTC). She led the group at times when needed. She knew the routines perfectly and participated in parades and activities around the city. She was also taught aviation there and was given the privilege to fly a plane from one city to the next with supervision. She earned 2 stripes and reached the Corporal ranking. It was there where she met the love of her life. He was a sergeant in the ROTC and led many groups.

Just imagine a freshman; thirteen, young, innocent, and easily impressionable. Freshman year is thrilling enough in itself but, this was also her first year in public school. Catholic school was strict and there wasn't any room to meet boys or do anything outside of school work. Public school was different. Everyone seemed free and alive. There was a vibrant atmosphere that was encircling this young girl who was getting her first taste of the real world.

The leader of the ROTC immediately took a notice on Lumi. He was seventeen, a senior and very handsome.

Every day was bringing something new and one day, that handsome senior that all the girls wanted was handing her a rose. "A rose for a rose," he told her. She could feel her heart hammering in her chest and the blood flushing from her cheeks. Was this actually happening? Never would she imagine that this man would take an interest in her. In a world where everyone ignored her, finally someone saw her.

He would walk her home from school nearly every day. It was perfect. He was someone she could look up to, someone who could protect her. She didn't have to be alone. She didn't have to work hard like her mother. She could be with this man. This man who was charming and smart. This man who was strong and lean. This man who had a job. This man who'd given her a rose. This man who would become her husband.

When she turned sixteen it only made sense that they married since he was going to the army and they had planned to go together. He could take care of her and they loved each other. Even though she was extremely smart and had A's in all her classes, she dropped out to get married. It was very common to leave school once you were married in those days. She didn't need her education. She had him. He was the love of her life and that's all she needed.

Here began another episode that marked her life.

This Journey Called Life Is Not Always Easy To Live, But The Opportunity To Do It The Best Way We Can And Know How To Do It, Is A Blessing That Goes Beyond Human Understanding

Chapter 2

THE BEGINNING

Pain is an indication that something must change...

Every cycle is initiated with a beginning...

Lumi's father wasn't involved with her courtship. He was always too sick to go anywhere and wasn't physically and mentally capable to get involved in what was happening in her relationship. Something I'm sure her boyfriend noticed. Her mother on the other hand, did not take a liking to her boyfriend. She seemed to know something that Lumi couldn't see. But Lumi didn't care. She didn't want to believe anything her mother had to say. After all, her own mother was spending her time with another man. How could she tell her she wasn't allowed to be with someone when she was being unfaithful herself?

She felt being with this guy was good for her. She needed him. So even when he showed signs of being abusive early on while they dated, she just ignored it. Everything would be fine one minute and then she would say something he didn't like or ask a 'stupid' question and he'd yell in her face. She can hardly even remember each altercation or what caused what reaction. It would seem to happen in the blink of an eye. A smack here, a shove there. "But things would get better once we married," she thought. She just had to get to that wedding.

Her uncle went out one night to meet with a prostitute. He went to the usual spot where he would meet her and discovered there was someone he knew there as well: his niece's fiancé. He immediately went to Lumi and confessed what he saw. "This isn't the one." He told her, "you are innocent. He's not good for you."

She rejected what her uncle saw. She couldn't believe it. It wasn't too long after her mother came back around saying "that man will make you miserable. Do not marry him." She remembers those words so clearly coming from her mother's mouth, but she refused to listen.

Her fiancé would be leaving for the army soon and so they married quickly at a church that her mother set up. The reception followed at her house. Though her mother didn't agree with her daughter's choice she didn't want to push her away—so she took care of every detail. There's a wedding picture of them where you can see the innocence in the young bride's eyes. The assurance that this was right. The groom, handsome and lean smiling gently. Lumi held onto that picture for many years. It now rests in her daughters' home for memory's sake.

She married before her older sister. She was the center of attention now. She had everything she wanted. The man, the dress, the love…

In the short time her husband was home before he left to the army, they moved in with his father and step-mother. "Those times were a hell for me," she said. She was standing in front his whole family when he slapped her. She doesn't quite remember what happened to be slapped like that. All she recalls from those moments was the intense shock and overwhelming embarrassment afterwards. She wanted to run home to her mother…but of course she stayed with his family. Her mother-in law didn't make things any easier for her. She wasn't welcoming or considerate of her at all. Not only did she have to walk on egg shells around her new husband but his mother as well.

After two months, he went to the army and demanded Lumi to stay with his step-mother. She planned on going to the army with him, but he never made the arrangements to take her. She agreed to stay but as soon as he left, she fled to her mother's house. About a month later, she discovered she was pregnant. This pregnancy changed her life. They wrote to each other constantly. While he stayed in the army, her mother took care of her like a princess. Though being at home was a relief, it came with its thorns too.

When it came time for Lumi to deliver her first child, her mother took her. In the waiting room to give birth, Lumi shared the room with another army wife whose husband asked for time off to see the birth of his first son. She couldn't help but feel neglected. Her husband decided to take the time off to go visit his brother as he was having sexual relationships with his wife—she would later discover, instead of visiting his first son.

Despite her husband ignoring her during this precious moment she describes her first pregnancy and birth as breath of fresh air. Medicine in the mist of her pain, rejection and abandonment. Her first born filled her emptiness. She experienced a honeymoon-like stage with her first son, affectionately known as Joey. He made her a mother. She looked at him every day in awe. He was so cute and chubby—the most beautiful creation God had made. He kept her sane and grounded through that time of pain and disappointment. God knew it was all too much for her and provided a way of escape for her.

He is a merciful God. He will always provide a form of escape.

Not long after Joey was born, her mother openly revealed she was in love with another man and divorced her father. Lumi found the news devastating. She suddenly had to meet the man who was coming in between her parents: Don Carlos. He worked with her mother for years and apparently was totally taken with her. He was married as well.

Her mother and Don Carlos had a funny relationship. He was extremely affectionate, always wanting to kiss on her and hug her meanwhile her mother was extremely sassy. She would push him away. She always had him around and cooked for him and practically looked after him. It was no denying they had something truly special. And despite their bond, at the end of the day she'd send him home to his wife.

Lumi wanted to hate her mother's mistress, but his gentle and caring persona made it hard. He was very kind to her and respectful of her space. Her sister however, till this day, found the entire situation infuriating. Don Carlos wanted to leave his wife and marry her mother instead, but her mother, despite being a spit fire, felt guilty and wouldn't go through with it. It would take years for her mother to fully come to terms with how her relationship affected another woman's life. She would be an old woman having lived her life before one day calling Don Carlos wife to truly apologize for messing around with her husband. His wife would cry and forgive her. And her mother would let the love of her life go after 50 or so years of being together.

After her son was six months old, her husband came to meet him. His son loved him instantly despite her husband not being very affectionate. He would go to the bars and clubs at night. He'd even come back a day later at times. During the day he worked odd end jobs here and there. They weren't financially stable on their own. Eventually, her mother bought them a condo, so they could move and be more comfortable.

He continued to not hang around much, gone most of the day and all night. One day Lumi stressed the importance of spending quality time with him. They were finally in their own place together and had a child. He should be home to help raise their son. He became furious. He didn't like to be challenged in any way by her. He put his hands around her neck as if he would strangle her to death. The look in his eyes was haunting and almost unhuman. She managed to get away and ran to the police fearing for her life. She left in such a panic she left her baby son behind. She never thought she would be capable of that. The police couldn't help her, so she ran to her mother's house.

The following day she found out he took Joey to his step-mother's house. He threatened her to leave him there if she didn't come back. She went to get him with tears in her eyes and her head hanging low.

It was torment. Looking back sometimes she doesn't understand how she dealt with the abuse or where she got the strength to deal with it. She found herself living a vicious cycle: SOMETHING HAD TO CHANGE.

She would wake up – take care of the baby – clean – cook – and then take care of her husband. The next day it would be the same thing all over again.

An abusive cycle can be born in every type of relationship. Unfortunately, when the person lives in the cycle of abuse, it becomes a normal lifestyle. There are mental and emotional ups and downs of the relationship that become mainstream in their lives. Many times, it becomes extremely difficult to leave these relationships for many reasons; fear of facing the future alone, fear of what would people say, and the reality of realizing that you are being abused.

This was the cycle Lumi lived for many years.

- Explosion
  He would mistreat her either with his hands or his voice.

- Remorse
  He'd come around and ask for her forgiveness and promise to not do anything like it again.

- Honeymoon Stage
  He'd make up for it by either being sweet to her or staying

home for a night or two. She'd believe things would get better.

- Tension

  Something in the air would seem off. He'd come home upset. He wouldn't come home at all. The baby was crying to loud. The food wasn't good enough…then he'd explode.

Chapter 3

"A NUTSHELL"

We Are Not Always Supposed to be Comfortable

The obsession of everything relating to one's self is a simple and concise way of defining narcissism…

Obviously, Lumi couldn't feel free to be herself when she lived with a man that everything had to revolved around him.

It's horrible to live in a world where your life is sucked out of you daily by constant manipulations of the soul. The time comes when you are so drained that you are no longer the same.

Your energy is drained, and your mental health is jeopardized.

When Joey was a year and two months old, she had her second child. Her husband had been medically discharged from the army at this point and continued to work odd end jobs here and there to support the family. Despite him working as best as he could there were times that she would go to her mother's house just so she could eat.

She focused on the excitement of her second child, affectionately known as Jay. Another handsome boy—such a joy for Lumi. She remarks that he was born with muscles. He looked so athletic. He had a lot of energy and was a happy baby. Now it was the three of them.

Her sons got along so well, always adventurous and making messes all over the house. It was her pleasure to raise and play with them. Their father never really spent time with them. He went to work, then to hang out and sometimes not return until the next day. She made sure he had warm food and clean clothes so when he returned, he could shower, change clothes, and eat.

By the time her sons were three and four years old her husband was invited to go to church with a friend. It was a Christian-Pentecostal church in Puerto Rico. He began attending and gave his heart to the Lord. It seemed he was committed and wanted to change his life around for the better, but since Lumi didn't trust him, she didn't want to go with him for a while.

One night there was a party celebrating his birthday and he refused to go because he had changed his lifestyle. Lumi however, out of rebellion, decided to go. She was quite the dancer—still is. When she got back home, she was afraid of what to expect from her husband. Normally she'd be expecting to receive a beating or at least a curse word or two. However, to her surprise, when she arrived, he received her with open arms and asked if she had a good time. She was shocked and realized a real change was happening. She began to believe in the same God he was believing in. The God that sent His Beloved Son to die on the cross and resurrected the third day for the salvation of this world.

She went to church and gave her heart to the Lord and began to serve the community whole heartedly. She remembers testifying on the miracles God had done in their marriage all over Puerto Rico. She finally found peace through God. Her marriage was flourishing. He wasn't going out at night. He was spending time in the house and being kind. They were both eager to learn more being the young Christians they were.

Not too long after, Lumi had her third child. She knew she was having a girl the moment she realized she was pregnant. It felt like another bonus for all the good going on in her life. By this point she had deeply desired having a daughter. Her third child affectionally known as Janna, was born. She was all over again in cloud nine. Her rosy cheeks and smile melted her heart. She was perfect. This woman was at the peak of her happiness.

Everything was going well until things for money became pressed. Her husband found himself mixed up with a gang and began selling drugs. His job involved taking the product and transferring it to different locations so it could be distributed. After seeing the kind of money being made in this business, he began stealing a portion of the product for himself and selling it on his own. He was making crazy amount of money and wasn't planning on slowing down until he was caught by his employers.

The man he was stealing from became aware. He was known for being a major killer in PR. Everyone involved in that world knew his name. Her husband caught wind that he was sent after him.

At this point Lumi was committed to the Lord. She was learning to rely on Him. She began to read the Word of God and had a hunger to learn more but, she found herself once again devastated in anguish. She felt hopeless. Her prayer life with God became stronger and stronger. She was learning about the miracles of God and how to live a life according to Gods Word. She thought something would change since she was praying; but nothing did. The more she wanted to go back to having the family she dreamed of, the unhappier she felt. The farther away her husband became.

In Matthew 12:43-46 it educates us not to go back to the mess He took you out of. Sin grows in progression. A drug addict didn't become an addict overnight. It's a progression of bad decisions that lead them to the addiction.

I was a substance abuse counselor for various years in one of the worst areas of The Bronx and Brooklyn, NY. My patients didn't start injecting heroin or snorting cocaine right away. All their stories started very similar. They started with being around the wrong crowd, smoking cigarette, smoking marijuana. Had beer then alcohol. They needed more, so they went on to the heavy drugs. Usually it started with a small portion and with time it grew to bigger portions. Causing even more chaos in their lives. Resulting in the loss of their children, jail, broken marriages etc.... All of them told me they had a way out before it got to rock bottom. Some stopped but started again and got worse. Every time they stopped and started again, it got worse and worse. Until they ended up in a place where they were mandated by the state to attend a program to be able to move on in their lives.

Lumi didn't realize it at the time, but God had a plan. He always does.

God has a plan. He always does.

Chapter 4

I NEEDED TO BE BORN…

Why God had my mother stay together with my father for so long?

Well, I needed to be BORN…

Before my father fled to NYC scared for his life, my mother got pregnant once more. When I was born, mom was at the lowest point of her life. She had three children already. She was okay not having any more. She contemplated getting an abortion because she didn't have the resources to take care of another child emotionally, mentally and financially. My father couldn't support a family of six. He was scared for his life. My mother couldn't conceive how she could take care of a fourth child. She was already feeling guilty exposing three children to the abuse, the violence and the inconsistencies he showed them. She didn't know what to do.

Somehow, she found the strength to go through with the pregnancy. When it was time to have me, as usual my father would drop her off at my grandmothers and she would take it from there. When my mother arrived at the hospital, she knew I was coming fast. She announced it and no one in the hospital believed her. She grabbed a nurse and screamed, "SHE'S COMING NOW". They rushed her to the elevator without a bed and she almost delivered me right there. She held on until they could place her on a bed. As soon as they laid down, I was born. It was another girl for her. When she saw me, she was so glad she didn't abort me. It filled her heart with joy and gratitude. It was everything she wanted in another girl. She thought, "My daughter, Janna has her companion baby sister, Jina" Her family was complete.

My father came to see me a few hours later and was glad as well. My mother thereafter, was forced by my grandmother to get an operation to stop her from having children. My mother wasn't in her right state of mind and would've had another child without even thinking. The stress my father put her under would've killed her had it not been for the four of us. She lived for us. We were her joy in the mist of darkness. She kept herself busy taking very good care of us. She pleased us in every way she could. As we grew older, she always sat down with us to advise us. She made sure we had warm breakfast, lunch and dinner. Our clothes were always washed, ironed, and put away. She bought us pets to entertain us and new clothes. We always looked stylish and put together.

As my brothers grew into their teenage years, she felt she lost a lot of her connection with them as they became more independent. My father pushed them to become men early on. Her boys felt greatly loved by her and protected to the best of her ability. But they had the unfortunate experience of knowing the limits of motherhood when it came to life under my fathers' rule. She did her best to jump in the middle of fights to protect them but she wasn't always successful.

I remember being around 8-9 years old, when my oldest brother Joey, flunked Jr. High. My father stormed into his room and beat him up like he was going to kill him. I sat there hearing my father screaming "How could you flunk school? You're stupid! You're stupid!" Repeatedly while my brother cried. My mother threw herself in between them and took some of the beating as well.

Thinking on it, my father was the top of his class in school. He had to be the best. He had to have the best. Did he think he failed somehow by not having a son who was the best? But Joey, just wasn't a school kid like my father. His talents were elsewhere. But that wasn't enough for my father.

There came a point, my mother confessed, that if I wasn't born, she would have killed herself. There came a time when it was just us supporting each other, loving each other, and encouraging each other. I was the only one there, morning, noon and night. Right now, although my mother cherishes all of her children, I'm the closest to her. Had I not been born…where would she be now?

There are times God uses the last person you'd expect to guide you and be there for you in your times of troubles.

I needed to be born for such a time like this. I came at a seemingly terrible point in my mother's life but, God knew I was necessary.

My mother made motherhood seem easy when she was raising us. She had everything in order. She never complained, got angry, cursed, or acted sad raising us. I grew up knowing nothing of what was transpiring behind closed doors. I never knew my father was unfaithful. I never knew about some of the things he did with my brothers. I didn't know how he manipulated so many situations that I found myself in. My mother covered me from so many things. And when I found everything out, I asked, "Why did you stay so long?"

Why I believe my mother stayed in the relationship with my father?…

My mother prayed for change. She never thought of divorce. The trauma of her parents getting a divorce resonated daily in her soul. She knew God hated divorce and strongly believed and hoped my father would be healed and restored. She held onto him because she believed it was what God wanted. She was never open to the fact that his infidelity gave her a way out of her torment.

She Had A Low Self-Esteem

She had a low self-esteem and was so wounded with her situation. She felt worthless. In front of everyone he acted as if he was the greatest husband but in private, he was a demon with her.

Self-Esteem is something dynamic, movable and changeable. We can have a high self-esteem in some areas of our lives and not in others. Some people are excellent in their jobs but may not be effective in other areas. Our self-esteem is the way we feel about ourselves as I discussed earlier. It is hard to believe our biggest battles are within us. *Our biggest battles are with our mind and the way we think. You are the first person that knows about your problems although you might not want to admit it.* Our self-esteem is one of the first ingredients and most important ingredient to feel good about who we are. Love always starts from within. *Loving oneself is so important to be able to effectively love your creator and your neighbor. The Bible says in Luke 10:27, "'Love the Lord your God with all your heart and with all your soul and with all your strength and with all your mind'; and, 'Love your neighbor as yourself.'"*

Self-esteem consist of valuing yourself and feeling you have internal resources *to be happy.*

Free Will…

God is a God of great mercy. God is a gentleman. He gave us free will.

In the mist of all the chaos my mother went through and the immense faith she had, she didn't realize at the time, we all have something called free will. God gave us the privilege to make our own decisions. We are not robots. It is up to us to make the right decisions. At the time this abuse was happening, my father was not choosing freedom. As much as God wanted to change him and answer my mother's prayers, it was ultimately up to my father to make those changes, not Gods. There were times my mother felt my father would change and it was good for a while, but then it would go back to the same thing. Even my mother had the choice to leave him, but her choice was to stay. The choice was not God's; it was there's.

Many times, we ask God to change a person, when we are the ones who need to change.

She was always blamed for everything that went wrong, and she would somehow take the blame. She did everything possible to please him, but he didn't change.

She never wanted her children to be raised without their father. So, she stayed. There were times when her children were glad, but times they wonder if it would've been better without him.

Not too long after I was born my father fled PR to get away from the man trying to kill him. He found himself in New York City where he decided this was his chance to start over.

CHAPTER 5

FACING REALITY

ANGER WILL TERMINATE THE DESTINY GOD HAS FOR YOU...

Right after I turned one years old, my mother, Lumi received a call from my father. He told her he was in NYC looking for work and a place to stay for the family. His better news was that he had returned to the church and was changing his life around again.

Out of excitement and hoping all will be well, she packed what she could with all us and left Puerto Rico to NYC. My father had found an apartment and made sure all of us would be taken cared of financially. We attended a local church and became involved in leadership. Our house was always packed with people and everyone loved us.

Though when all the guests left the house, the demeanor would change. My father's behavior was something everyone would be afraid of. We all had to be careful around him behind closed doors.

I always saw my father as an angry man. He seemed to be angry all the time when he was alone with the family. When he got home, we all ran to our room. We didn't want to get screamed at. He always found something wrong and had all of us running around trying to fix it. He was always angry.

As I look back on my life and see how I inherited his strong work ethic, I wonder, what if he was always tired and didn't know it? We all know, no sleep can get us into a bad mood. Maybe combining no sleep with not knowing how to express any other feelings but anger caused him to be angry all the time? This is a bad combination.

Men are told since they are very young, "Don't cry, men don't cry." "Suck it up." They are taught very young not to show any emotions. However, for some reason, it's okay to show anger. It's almost like anger demonstrates manhood in our culture. As if anger is not an emotion but a way of defining manhood.

Knowing what I know now, I wonder if my father growing up without a mother caused this anger. My father lost his mother when he was 4 years old to a terminal illness. He remembers kissing her in her casket and never forgetting how beautiful she was. His step-mom and aunts mistreated him. He was beaten every single day by his step mother and his aunts were no comfort when they were around. He doesn't even remember why. He says he was a good boy. A normal boy that liked to play pranks on people but, normal non-the-less. He did extremely well in school. He was the valedictorian for Elementary, JHS, HS, College and Bible Seminary. He was a leader. He was well liked. Everyone wanted to be around him in school. My father was the type to defend his friends. He was put in charge of the ROTC since he was a Freshmen in High School. Unfortunately, he didn't bring that greatness into his marriage and parenting.

Anger destroyed the beautiful destiny God had for him while with his family.

Being the youngest of four, I always felt all my siblings and parents protected me. I felt protected and secure most of the time. Out of everyone in the family, I believe I was the most sheltered. I never really knew what was going on or being said. In many ways I'm extremely thankful for this, although I still experienced trauma that until today I can't fathom how I survived them.

My first remembrance of my father's anger was at the early age of 2-3 years old. I remember having a security blanket that I held onto everywhere I went. Although my mom cleaned it all the time, it bothered my father that I had it on me often. So, one day, he yanked my security blanket off me and threw it down the incinerator. He was such an authoritative figure to me. He was the boss in my eyes. I could see him now as he walked to the incinerator and told me "no more." What my father said, was what we all did. Without negotiating, without questioning, without bending the rules. If my father said it, it was a commandment.

My mother always gave him that authority and we all respected him at the upmost level. But that didn't stop the pain during times when it felt so personal. I remember my mother taking me in her arms and assuring me that everything would be okay.

There was another time my father came home annoyed about something and we happen to be playing in the living room at the wrong time. My father screamed at all of us and took my brothers' bikes and threw them out of the window because they were in the middle of their room. Afterward he made my brothers go down and get them before anyone noticed. We lived on the second floor of project buildings in Spanish Harlem, in NYC.

My father was always working from sunrise to sundown. My sister would get very sad when he wasn't around. She was about 4 years old or so and she would sit by the window and wait for my father to come home. He was the provider and my mom stayed home taking care of all of us.

Even when they weren't pastoring, they always seemed to have a spotlight on them. I remember being so proud of them. They were always in front of the church leading some group or organization.

Our typical day of entertainment was playing in the house. We would play church in the living room. My brothers played instruments and preached, and my sister and I would play the tambourine and sing. We all loved it. My mother always sat us down and prayed for us and with us. She taught us the right values and disciplined us. Most importantly, she taught us the word of God.

My mother didn't work the first 4 years of my life. I thank my father for that. He provided all our needs financially. Once I went to Kindergarten, my mother had jobs working from home while we went to school. Dinner was always ready when we returned. She was so loving and nurturing, always kissing and hugging us. I never saw my mother angry. She was always the peace maker.

My mother was a teacher in the church and in the home. I used to love to listen to her. I remember my mother cooking 4-5 course meals every day except Sundays. We would go out to eat or buy food. I loved it since it broke the routine and felt like a treat. Having people over often also gave way to having my parents teach me to serve. I knew from an early age how to be polite and a good host. Those skills came to my benefit in my adulthood. I thank them for that.

Despite the random outburst from my father I thought my childhood was blessed and it was. I had everything I needed. Even in a bad situation I was still living a better life than most.

One thing I had a hard time getting over was how my father was affectionate to me in front of people but when no one else was around he'd reject my love. He was always so busy doing something for the church or work. There were times I would want to hug or kiss him, and he would tell me, "go over there," and not respond to my affections. I felt I was only good for getting things for him like his shoes, water, or whatever he needed. I always listened to him. There were even times, he would call me to do things for him while I was sleeping. Although what he wanted was a short distance from him and long distance from me, I would gladly do it anyway.

I wanted to be daddy's little girl like my mother with her father. In those times I thought it wasn't such a big deal. I just thought he was busy. I knew deep inside he loved me. I grew up with that mentality of always serving him. I accepted the role of willingly serving everyone around me without question.

I was still young when I was molested. A man came over to paint our walls and it was nothing new to me to have a stranger in our home. He asked me to help so I did, since we were always serving everyone anyway. He needed to pick me up so I could reach the parts of the wall he couldn't reach. I was a loving little girl and didn't think anything of what he asked. When he picked me up, he grabbed me in between my legs. I felt violated immediately. My mother came in and noticed it right away and told me to go to my room.

Because of fear, my mother didn't say anything. I felt she blamed me for what happened. I know that if my mother told my father, my father would have taken the situation into his hands, literally. My father didn't play around. My mother stayed quiet to keep the peace, but her silence also made me feel like I did something wrong.

It would be years later when that moment would ever be brought up again. To my surprise my mother didn't blame me for the situation but cautioned me not to go near strangers unless approved by her. I understood the power behind a parent safe guarding a child then. Sure, my mother didn't go to any authorities or even to my father, but she stopped it when it happened. She watched me closely ever since.

There are many ways of mistreating children, including neglect as part of emotional abuse.

Verbal abuse is a real thing.

The word of God is extremely clear about the dangers of an angry man. Proverbs 22:24 says: **24** "Do not make friends with a hot-tempered person, do not associate with one easily angered,"

Proverbs 29:22 says:" **22** An angry person stirs up conflict, and a hot-tempered person commits many sins."

I know this is very difficult to hear, especially if you're in a marriage or in a relationship with someone who is verbally abusive. My heart is not to hurt anyone but to simply make you aware of the word of God.

It is not the will of God for you to be in a relationship that's verbally abusive or is governed by religiosity. Those angry words of criticism destroy your self-image and self-esteem. To be submissive in your marriage doesn't mean you need to tolerate any verbal abuse or any type of abuse, no matter what happens.

The word of God teaches the verbally abused that in no way you should be subject to any type of verbal or physical abuse. NEVER!

God loves you.

He says in His word:

Psalms 34:18, "**18** The Lord is close to the brokenhearted and saves those who are crushed in spirit.

Chapter 6

FINDING MY OWN FAITH

The Life of a PK (Pastor's Kid)

Once we had settled into our home in NYC, we began attending a church in Spanish Harlem and were very committed to the church and to the work of God. My father was changing again for the better and my mother was so happy and hoping for the best. They were serving the community with passion and devotion.

Around the time the I was 6 years old my parents were asked to pastor a church in The Bronx, NY.

There's such a thin line between getting wisdom and observing the good versus observing the bad and the ugly in a pastor's home...

My first experience with God was so vivid, that I still feel as if it was yesterday.

We attended a church in upper Manhattan on the west side. I believe I was about 4 years old when I felt the baptism of the Holy Spirit for the first time. I remember my sister being fervently prayed for on the alter by the evangelist. It seemed as if the whole church knew she would be baptized with the Holy Spirit right there and then. Everyone was focused on her. All their hands were extended to her and the evangelist was praying blessings over her and asking her to praise the Lord out loud and to feel free to worship. I was so happy for her that she would finally feel God in that way. "What a privilege," I said to myself. "This is the greatest moment of her life. My sister is going to be filled with the baptism of the Holy Ghost." She was the youngest child ever in my eyes. My sister was always the chosen one and I was her shadow. I wanted to be like her. She was a leader. The president of the kids and always in charge. I was proud of her. I felt she deserved to be blessed. I was so very happy for her.

My mother had so much to do with the way I felt in that moment. I remember my mom made serving God so attractive. She made us feel on top of the world. She always told us we were chosen by God to serve Him. At least for me, I felt privileged. Better than the average child. I even knew in that young age that I was a child of a King. Nothing could break me. I could do everything through Christ who strengths me. I knew it. I embraced it and walked in that Word.

So, there it was, Janna got filled with the Holy Spirit of God. She began to jump up and down. The church went wild. Everyone was so excited to see a young child in that blessing. It was at that time when I also felt the presence of God. All my hairs stood up. I wanted to jump up and down and run all over the church. I was filled with the joy of the Lord. I didn't want to stop. I was in complete praise and worship to God.

I remember once the service was over, I didn't want to leave. I asked my mom if we could go to another church that was open later. She looked at me strangely but understood I didn't want to leave the presence of God. Despite me saying something silly like that, she listened to me and made me feel like my voice mattered. I will never forget that night.

A few years later, my parents were called to pastor. The next thing I knew we were in a new church. After seeing my parents teach Sunday School and lead the youth, it wasn't new to me to see my parents in charge. They were always in the lead and being followed by many. I grew up thereafter being a pastors' kid.

For a long time, I felt subject to deal with the critical eyes of others and what's worse was my behavior constantly being judged by many. But it wasn't just the church members I had to be perfect for; it was my father as well.

He had an extremely high standard for all of us. We needed to be perfect 24/7 to satisfy him, and even then, he'd find something to scream at us about. We were all well behaved kids. We were involved in the church and everyone always gave us compliments about how good we looked and how mature we were. But it was never enough.

I was 8 or 9 years old when I was extremely embarrassed by my father in front of the whole church. I was sitting in my seat chewing gum but, paying attention to the preaching. My father noticed and stopped his sermon right in front of everyone and yelled "Throw away your gum!" He waited for me to get up and spit it out in front of the whole church. I was humiliated. After service, my father brought me into his office and spanked me.

The way we were raised in church was, what people consider now, very old fashioned. Girls couldn't wear pants or anything above the knee, and even that was considered risqué. No jewelry, no make-up. We weren't allowed to take pride in the way we looked. If we went to the beach, then we went in long sleeve shirts and ankle length skirts.

It created this sense in me that I wasn't meant to be beautiful. I was ugly and needed to hide herself. I felt discouraged from feeling pretty.

But despite some of the downfalls of being in the church I still truly loved going. I was unashamedly a church girl. My sister and I loved serving in church, singing on the pulpit and leading groups in the church. I loved going out and giving tracks and praying for people. When the church would block off certain streets to have service outside, I prayed for people passing by. The older I got the more responsibility and leadership roles I took on in the church. My youth was surrounded by church and God, and I don't regret it.

I know however, I had a very different experience from my brothers. They grew up different from my sister and I. My father put a lot pressure on them to be men and to grow up fast. From what I saw growing up, he wanted my brothers to be in ministry and become preachers like him. However, there was much more going on.

My father had irrational fears that his sons would turn out weak if he wasn't hard on them. He would tell them very aggressively and vulgarly that he didn't want them turning out gay. And to ensure that his sons would be men, he coaxed them into getting with virgin girls, looking at women, and knowing exactly what to do with them.

The very perverse issues my brothers struggled through while growing up, such as being addicted to pornography as early as the age of three years old, was introduced to them by their father. I see myself growing up so innocently back then, handing out tracks and inviting people to church, not knowing my brothers were protecting us from the vilest things. In part, I understand why they were so aggressive toward guys who took an interest in my sister and I. They knew what the minds of men could think of. They knew what it felt like. They knew we shouldn't be any part of it.

None of them should have.

My father's violence trickling down to my brother and sister mostly. My brother used to get so angry he would hit us at times when we didn't follow his rules. One day while he was taking care of us, he felt my sister disrespected him. He got so angry that he slapped her. He regretted it so badly, he pushed the wall and broke his wrist. My older sister was abusive towards me. There was so much violence going on, she doesn't recall some of the abuse.

There was one time, my father got so mad at my oldest brother for talking back to him, that he threw a key at him. It hit my brother on the back of the head and got stuck there. When my brother pulled it out, he revealed a heavy stream of blood coming from his skull. My mother jumped in and had to rush him to the hospital.

My brother's lives in the church was a complete 180 from my sister and I. It was competition between my father and my brothers. Who could get the most girls? Because my father was so open with the women from church, they would divulge themselves sexually to my brothers as well. And my father egged them on like it was a horse race. But any time one of them was caught by a member of the church, my father was the first to discipline them.

They would sit during the service and if my brothers weren't on the pulpit doing music, helping preach or apart of any of the activities, everyone knew what had happened. It was meant to be embarrassing. They were meant to sit in shame. I thinks about it now and I don't understand how putting someone under that kind of shame would ever make anyone want to repent and return to church but, that was how they grew up.

My problem never really fell with the church. It was my father's bitterness toward us.

The older my sister and I got, the worse things got between the men in our house and the men in the world. Guys couldn't even look at us without getting our brothers riled up. My brothers and father protected us to the highest level. If you wanted to talk to us, you had to go through them. It had its charms when we were young but as a teenager and young adult, we knew it was a bit much.

I was about 17-18 years old when a guy I liked passed by the house with a friend to show off his new car. I had no idea he was coming by. When he knocked on the door, my father opened it. He called me once they asked for me. When I came over, I immediately knew my father was upset. He thought I had invited them over without his permission.

Dating was tricky in my house. Once 18 years old, we were allowed to go out on dates in groups or with supervision. Never alone and definitely with approval from my father beforehand. I was obedient to my parents' rules however my father always seemed to suspect I would sneak around. He was so sure he would catch me with some lies. Now I see he was only judging me due to his lifestyle and my brother's lifestyle.

I remember him telling my mom one day, "if you don't watch them, (referring to my sister and I), they will come out as prostitutes."

If a guy wanted to visit us, he could only do it on Saturday at a certain time and with supervision. We would sit in the living room with the rest of the family and watch a movie or hang out altogether. Maybe have a few minutes of alone time as we walked to the door, earshot of our father, but that's it.

Once my friends left, I went to the living room to watch television. It was a hot Wednesday night. I turned on the fan and directed it to me. I wasn't even thinking anything was wrong when I suddenly felt my father's hands on me. He came out of nowhere, punching me as hard as if I was a man. He didn't hold anything back. He screamed saying I didn't have the fan circulating around the living room. He repeated something to that effect while he beat me until my mother came in to stop him.

I thought he was going to kill me. My mother got in the way before he smashed a porcelain doll over my head. Again, my mother got hit for us.

I ran to the kitchen planning my escape. I was for sure leaving the house. I was not going to live in these conditions, especially being innocent. My mother went to the kitchen to calm me down. She sat with me for hours until I was calm and ready to go to sleep.

I confronted him in my twenties about that incident. He looked at me first as if he didn't remember, then he said, "forget about that, why are you bringing it up?" and walked away like nothing.

He didn't even acknowledge what he did or apologized to me. I looked at him and said, "I forgive you." The day went on and no acknowledgement was made on the conversation.

My sister shares a similar story. While joking around together in the living room with our father, things became violent. It became a tickle fight between them—just silly fun and games. She said they were both laughing. "I thought we were just playing." But suddenly, either she tickled him too hard by mistake or did exactly nothing at all, our father's expression changed. He suddenly grabbed my sister's head and smashed it into the wall with all his might. Thankfully the walls in our apartment were paper thin and no real damage was done but the impact left her dazed.

She didn't understand where the aggression came from. They were just hugging and tickling each other just a moment ago and now he was smashing her face in the wall and yelling at her to get away. She snapped for a moment and after she got undazed, she ran into her room and tried to jump out the window. "I wanna die! I wanna jump!" She screamed and our mother was the only one there to hold her back.

From the experiences I've had being a pastor's kid, I've began to develop a passion to be able to impact pastor's children. Amongst many other groups in the community, my main passion has been this group.

In my case, alongside the abuse we were facing at home, we also faced it in the church. Why do people attack pastor's children so much? Why are people so bitter against them? Why people expect more from them, than from other kids? Why are they focused on them to see any failures of the pastors or to single them out and embarrassed them in front of others? Why?

I can name a few things, but one of the main reasons why I felt to write this book, is to illuminate and show that you can become free from these struggles and burdens.

Real envy and jealousy in people do exist. People don't want you to succeed. It's even sadder to say that it exists in religious circles. Average people don't want you to move on. They want you to stay a victim and be in the bottom of the barrel. If you want to have a lot of friends, always talk about your problems, always be a victim and pity yourself. These are situations people relate too. Once you overcome all that pain and let it go, decide to move on, then you're alone. No one wants to back you up. You lose friends.

One thing I've learned is that people do not determine your future. Don't let the pain of this world determine your future either. Let your pain determine the destiny in God. You must learn how to live through criticism when you are the center of attention and live with the pressure people put on you to be better than the rest of the children/people in the church.

I understood these challenges are not only for Christian leaders but for every Christian parent. It's to be a leader in your home who teaches your children the Word of God and most importantly be an example of all you teach by faith.

For a long time, I felt subject to deal with the critical eyes of others and what's worse was my behavior being constantly judged by other.

Let's stop expecting more from pastor's children's than from other children of the church.

As I've seen pastors' kids abused by the church, I've also seen pastor's kids taking advantage of the church and demanding things that frankly they have not earned. We must be very careful that we don't automatically feel entitled because our parents are the leaders. The parents are the leaders, not the children. Leadership is earned and not inherited.

As the parents, I would strongly encourage pastors to take out time with their children when they are young. Speak to them about how they might be feeling. Educate them about life not just the church. Church is just an extension of what the real world is like. As much as we want to believe that everyone is holy in the church, the reality is the church is a hospital, as my last Pastor used to say. We are all sick and are seeking healing. You find everyone in a hospital as you would in a church. We all need to understand that you will not be liked by everyone.

Pastors speak to your children like a father and not a pastor. Don't preach to them, have conversations with them. Don't use the Bible as a punishment or judgement. Use it to show them the love of God. Spend time with them as you would the church.

GOD – FAMILY – THEN THE CHURCH (BUSINESS)

Educate yourself not to impose a ministry on your child if they are not called. Avoid nepotism in the church. This is not a business you can pass down, and even with a business you need to be educated and earn your position. This is ministry. Just because they are family, it doesn't mean they are called to pastor or be in a certain position because you choose to put them there.

PK's need to learn leadership skills and educate themselves in whatever calling God has given them. This is not a hand me down. These are God's people we are serving. This is why we see lots of PK's out of church, not valuing the ministry or position God has given them. When things are given easy, there is no value, no appreciation, and no struggle to keep what they have. Just like a business ran by a second generation who are entitled, and everything has been handed to them; without hard work, commitment and dedication, the business goes down the drain.

There are those who have reached positions of authority in whatever area of society who have abused of it in public and in private with their families.

Authority is always subject to abuse.

Chapter 7

NARCISSISM & RELIGION

It Gets Worse Before It Gets Better

Let's get back to my mother's story...

Lumi and her husband pastored for 10 years in The Bronx. A lot of great memories were created despite the bad. The ministry was flourishing. There was growth happening all over the place. They were side by side growing, a neighborhood, a village, a whole Borough. People came to the church from all over NYC to be blessed by God. The music was spectacular, and the preaching's were even better. We saw miracles and wonders in this church. It was truly amazing.

Lumi continued to run the home and run the ministry with her husband without a hair misplaced on her head. I looked at her with so much admiration back then, not even realizing she was barely hanging on.

As her oldest son, Joey, became of age to work, he was encouraged to get a job. So he did. The issue was, that he had to work on Sundays. This was a no, no in this household. Sundays, was church time. No bending the rules. No negotiating. Lumi's husband was furious he had to go to work on Sundays. The legalistic mentality and teachings at the time were so powerful that nothing else mattered, only following the rules. Her husband put his foot down and threw him out the house. Lumi was devastated. She didn't know how to stop it. She was in the middle as usual. She loved her son and feared her husband. She desperately pleaded for Joey to stay and her husband to change his mind, but there was no other option. Joey moved out and started to find his own way in the world. Her first true love was gone.

Narcissism and Religion

What do religious people and narcissistic people have in common?

Why are they this way?

Religion like culture, evolved during the years. It is impossible to understand the origin and function of different religions without understanding who we are as human beings.

Narcissism seems to be very common and normal in our society—today more so than ever.

Why are many religious leaders narcissistic?

Narcissistic say, "I am the only one. I want a different treatment. I am unique. Others are beneath me. I am the only special one." They love themselves more than God.

The religious leader believes he is someone superior as well. The same as the narcissist, the religious person loves to have followers, power, attention, and special privileges. As a preacher, one has all the above. It is very easy to take advantage of people when you're in power and forget that your talents, your grace and favor comes from God and from Him alone.

Many people in power fall in this trap of believing the lie that the influence they have come from their own strength. They feel they are indispensable. They feel they can get away with anything and no one would ever find out. They mistake God's grace and favor with their own abilities. It happens in every walk of life. Being a pastor, a boss, a business man or a politician. They use the gifts God gave them for their own fulfillment and gratification; instead of giving all the glory to God. It all comes from our Creator, and Him alone. Humbleness comes from understanding where the power comes from. Pride comes when you're blinded from that truth.

After 10 years, her husband took a year sabbatical from the church. Everyone thought it was year sabbatical but in reality, he was told by the leaders of the association of churches he belonged to, he had to step down. Lumi tried to cover for him as much as she could but, some people had given evidence of his infidelity. He had to leave.

Lumi remembers sitting in that office while her husband was being outed and feeling the office closing in on her. She nearly fainted. The world as she knew it was caving in on her and she didn't know what to do.

She questioned her husband about what he was being accused of and he denied it all. She had dealt with enough, but she didn't know how to get out. She felt trapped. She felt she had already lost her first born and now she was losing her church. The place where she felt free. The place where she felt safe. Where she had dedicated so many hours and poured her heart and soul into. She was so angry, but held it all in. She didn't want her children to know anything. She did everything she could to protect them from the truth for as long as she could.

She prayed and cried out to God to fix it all. She prayed for her older son every night for protection and guidance as she felt her hands were tied with the situation. She knew her other son wasn't making good decisions either. She prayed for him too.

My sister and I didn't know what was truly happening. We just knew that we suddenly lost all of our best friends and church family and we had to find a way to move forward.

Here started episodes of extreme anxiety and fear for Lumi. From the episode she experienced in the office at the church, she began to fear being in closed spaces. She couldn't lock the doors, go in elevators, pass bridges, or go in tunnels and subways. She became claustrophobic.

There's a chemical imbalance that happens in your brain when you cannot understand and are overwhelmed with the events you're going through. This chemical imbalance causes trauma; which is defined in the dictionary as a deeply distressing or disturbing experience. This results in extreme anxiety, fear, feelings of rejection, worthlessness, abandonment amongst low self-esteem and low self-image.

She remembers going to the doctor and sharing her symptoms. Her doctor gave her a prescription to see a psychologist and a psychiatrist. She was encouraged to take medication for anxiety and depression and make sure she got counseling. Lumi looked at the prescription, contemplating what she would do...

CHAPTER 8

WHATEVER IT'S HIDDEN IS MEANT TO BE DISCLOSED…

Mark 4:22 says, "For whatever is hidden is meant to be disclosed, and whatever is concealed is meant to be brought out into the open."

During the year sabbatical, Lumi's husband was low key. They all attended another church to stay active serving the community. Knowing her husband's heart was set on pastoring again, Lumi went back to the assembly and asked if he can pastor after the year was up. The assembly loved Lumi and knew she had a pure heart. Because she vouched for him, the assembly decided to give him another church. This time in Brooklyn, NY.

They start pastoring again. The church starts growing and the whole family starts working for the benefit of the community. At this time, Joey finds himself back with the family. Lumi was finding happiness again. Joey had met a young lady with a new born child that gave him shelter while he was homeless. Because Joey didn't love her, he asked his dad to let him move back in the house. But he advised to Joey was, "marry her." He was living with her and it was the right thing to do. Joey's heart was to serve the church, do things right, be faithful to God, be with his family, play his guitar and participate in the development of the church. So, he married the woman and helped raise her son as his own. The whole family embraced her son as their own flesh and blood.

Then a huge highlight in Lumi's life happened. Her first grandchild was born. The most beautiful granddaughter in her eyes. She was over joyed. The first of her next generation. She didn't know what else to do for her but give her all the love and necessities she could ever need. Everything was about her grandbaby. Lumi was overwhelmed by her. She wasn't a mother anymore, her grandbaby made her Grand.

Her husband was doing well again next to Lumi and the church flourished. Around a year after pastoring, God spoke to Lumi's heart to warn her husband about a huge struggle that was coming. Due to the way he was with her, he didn't take her advice. Instead, he exploded screaming, "who do you think you are advising me." He felt she had no right to advise him or warn him.

Lumi almost believed the lie. Maybe she didn't have the right to advise him. But she knew the relationship she had with God. She knew what God had told her. She prayed hard her husband would be able to overcome the next thing that came his way.

A few months passed from the time she had given her husband the word she received from God, when he started acting very strange around the house. This time, everyone in the household was very aware something was seriously wrong.

She remembers the night her husband didn't sleep at the house. Everyone was confused. Where was her husband? She remembers the exact date, October 10th, 1995. She already knew what was going on and with who it was going on with, but she was holding on. She thought, "oh no it's happening again." "How am I going to fix this or make this right?" Lumi wanted to be everything for her husband. Her deepest desire was to please his every need. But how could she? when she was constantly abused verbally, emotionally, psychologically and sometimes physically. She suffered daily for her children's well-being and if that wasn't enough she had to make sure everything ran smoothly in the home, with her children and the church. She was physically, emotionally and psychologically drained daily. She would get up every morning starting over again and doing everything in her power to please her husband.

Her husband however, didn't see that. His desires laid elsewhere. He didn't even want to hide it at this point. His lust for this women took over his desire to pastor, be a husband, be a father and most importantly be the man God had created him to be. He seemed proud of himself.

Her older daughter, Janna caught her father one day making himself up in the mirror in the hallway. She knew what was going on. She could see it on his face. And this time, she was too angry to let it slide.

You slept with her right?" She glared at him.

He turned to her without a hint of surprise and smirked at her smugly. They both knew who she was talking about.

"So, you did. You slept with her." she didn't want to believe it but, it was all too plain to see at this point. This man who she looked up to, admired, feared and respected didn't have so much as an ounce of shame.

"Why don't you love mommy?" was a question she'd ask him often in private. There was never a good reason. A haunting question without any real answers to give.

Papi why don't you love mommy?

For years this woman prayed for a change in her husband.

Papi why don't you love mommy?

She washed his clothes and cooked his food.

Papi why don't you love mommy?

She gave him healthy children and raised them.

Papi why don't you love mommy?

She supported his ministry and despite knowing he was fooling around with other women she covered his tracks so he wouldn't be ridiculed.

Papi why don't you love mommy?

She backed him up when the church pointed their fingers at him. She followed him from her homeland. She left her mother behind. She left it all behind for this man who handed her a rose.

Papi why don't you love mommy?

And she took the rose and held it tight, despite its thorns. Despite its faults.

Papi why don't you love mommy?

It was never about him not loving Lumi. It was about him loving himself more. More than his wife, more than his children and more than his God.

In the end the sin wasn't just the sex. It was the pride.

He came forward about the affair he was having with this woman. To everyone's surprise, ***it was his oldest son wife***. He didn't care what anyone thought anymore. He didn't want to hide it. He'd been sneaking around with her and he wanted it to be official between them. It was a disgrace for the whole family. Everyone was in awe. He was 20+ years her senior. This woman had no shame. She was as open about it as he was. It was a stab to the heart.

Lumi had embraced this woman as her own daughter. Taught her how to be a mom. Helped her grow up and take care of her two children. She showed her how to have a clean home and educated her in the beauty of being a woman of God and this is how she repaid her.

Believe it or not Lumi still didn't consider divorcing him. She thought he would come back—he always did. A few months passed and he did try to come back but, it didn't work out. The corrupted relationship he was in wrapped him right back in.

The family was ostracized from the church. The same church they were building up, leading in and worshipping in. Once again, they lost their friends, best friends and church family.

All financial ties from her husband were cut off. It all went to his new woman. He did pay the rent a few short months after but demanded authority as if he was still the man of the house. Lumi was not accepting it anymore. He had to leave if he was going to stay with her. Lumi thereafter, didn't so much as get a dime. She had no medical insurance; no money, no financial stability, she had nothing.

Lumi's oldest daughter, Janna was enraged. Her well-spoken, mild mannered daughter had had it. Without even thinking one night she went out for a walk.

Janna knew exactly where this woman lived and what time she would be home. "I was going to beat her up." Janna said. "I was going to knock on her door and beat her up right there." She walked all the way to where her father's mistress lived and just as she was getting close to her street, she happened to pass by a church that was conveniently having a worship service with its doors wide open.

"I could hear the music playing and I could hear the preacher praying in tongues. I knew who the preacher was too. He was a friend of mine."

She got stuck standing right outside the church doors unable to move forward. Her house was just a few more blocks down. "It was like the Holy Spirit saying, 'No' and I couldn't go. I turned around and walked all the way back home."

All of Lumi's children were angry, destroyed and lost all respect and admiration for their father. Lumi's final straw came when her oldest son, Joey came to the house devastated that his ex-wife was trying to take his daughter away. Her first grandbaby. Lumi's heart was broken even more if it was possible. She loved her grandbaby and was with her every day. She missed her grandbaby so much. When Joey cried out to her to please get a divorce, she finally did.

When her husband finally left the house for good, there was such an emptiness in all their hearts. They felt lost. "What do we do now?", they all said. Everyone that they thought was their church family, was nowhere to be found. No phone calls, no visits, no concerns about them. Nothing. Everyone left them. The people they knew and invested time in, their family, their friends, their best friends, were all gone. They were all alone. The life they lived was ripped out under them from one day to another. Only one leader of the association of churches they attended called Lumi, the national secretary at the time.

Joey moved on pretty quickly to a new wife and her other son, Jay had his own life. Jay had also met someone who he was starting his life with. Lumi only had her two daughters left but life as they knew it, was gone. Their whole lives revolved around the church. They lost everyone again and they had nothing to do with it.

Lumi lost it for a bit. She confessed she went through a very dark time. She thought, "is this the only thing life has to offer me?" She didn't know what to do. She lost her marriage, ministry, friends and life as she knew it. She was suffering this all by herself. She was alone, lonely, desperate, confused, angry, bitter, depressed and to top it off, she had multiple anxiety attacks daily.

I have to add; the life of a pastor's wife is a very lonely one. Who could she trust? Who could she speak too? When she told her family in Puerto Rico, they told her, "I knew this was going to happen, why didn't you leave him sooner?" They just made her feel worse.

Right before everything came out to the light, Lumi had fasted for three days. She was praying and pleading to God to fix her marriage. Then everything got worse.

Sometimes things get worse before they get better. I know now that if this didn't happen to Lumi, she would not be free today. She would not be living the best days of her life. She didn't know it at the time, but she had to learn on her own. She had to learn to trust God through it all. She had to lean on Him in her darkest hour so that He could bring her to her brightest day. It wasn't meant to happen the way she wanted it to happen. She had to learn to accept that.

It took Lumi a whole year to speak about what happened. She was unable to communicate the pain and disappointment she felt. She never wanted her children to see their father any other way but the King of the castle. The only answer for her at the time was to keep it in. Bottle it inside. She felt somehow it would all go away. "Everything will get better. It always does somehow," she felt.

Things did get better but not always in the way she expected it and in the timing she requested it. Despite it all, God had a plan.

Lumi did some things she wasn't proud of trying to let go of the pain and sorrow she was feeling. She temporarily forgot about her God. Questioned the situation, why me? What did I do? Why aren't you saving my marriage? There's nothing impossible for you Lord, why can't you save this marriage? What she didn't realize at the time was that God is not going to change someone that doesn't want to change. God doesn't force Himself upon us. He gives us free will. God will not overrule your choices.

God will not overrule your choices…

As it was her husband choice to sin, it was also Lumi's choice to stay. Sometimes the hardest choice to make is not to make change but to leave.

It was time for Lumi to stop being the victim and become the victor.

From Lumi's diary…

"My God is my shield, my pastor, my friend, and my true love. I always remained praying, fasting, and refuging myself in His presence and His word. Only God gave me the strength to move forward.

To live with him was to make sure all his needs were met. Everything had to benefit him. I never thought about his behavior affecting me in every area of my life. His behavior in the home was very different from the one outside of the home. His goal was always to control me and his family…we were his victims. When problems came; I was to blame, I had to change, it was always my fault.

The truth is that to live with a religious narcissist means to live with a liar. It's to live with someone whose values do not match up with their behavior. They live a false image of what it is to live like Jesus. Like politicians, who live a different life that they are campaigning about or like a boss who is mandating everyone to behave or perform a certain way, when they are not.

What was the point of emotionally abusing me, while in church he treated me great? Faith is not a status but a result of having a personal relationship with God. Jesus wants us to have things clear and human, not narcissistic.

A philosopher said, 'Everything that is born from ego, even with the best intention, will not flourish but increase the craziness of the world.'

I began to feel loneliness, low self-esteem, depression and anxiety. I didn't know how to behave or who to be. I needed to be careful as he was extremely vulnerable to any changes of behavior that I made. He made it clear that he was better than me and he was doing me a favor by being with me.

My ex-husband was a narcissist not egoistical. The difference is the egoism is the tendency of only worrying about oneself and not the needs of others while narcissism is being the center of the world, serving but for their own interest without compassion or empathy. The egoistic person doesn't create victims while the narcissistic does. I was my ex-husbands victim. He attacked my self-esteem, my confidence and my self-belief. It took me time to understand the problem. I lived many experiences with him. Not only verbal abuse but sexually too with adultery. I knew when he had another woman. The reality was that infidelity wasn't as important to me, as raising my children with their father, until it happened repeatedly. It had to stop when it directly affected my children. Living this life makes you take the fault for everything, even if you had nothing to do with it.

There were many times I've wondered what I was thinking when I married him. Many told me not to do it, including my mom and uncles. Then, there were other times when I blamed myself and mentally told myself I needed to be more understanding. I needed to give him space. I needed to watch what I said so he wouldn't get angry. I needed to keep it to myself when he wasn't treating me right. WHY? I always thought I was doing something wrong and was the cause for his infidelity.

I learned to please him. To live with simplicity and to control my moments of emotional confusion and chaos. All couples have their ups and downs? I would think. He provided financially, my children had a father, he put a roof over their head, he occasionally gave me gifts and we had a huge church family. I thought, I could deal with it. But even with that and all my changes, he would still make comments that I didn't understand him.

To live with my ex-husband was extremely difficult. He didn't only think he was special, but he thought he was the most important person in the world. He thought he was the most handsome, so consequently he wanted more attention. The reality is that now I understand that the narcissist and/or abuser is not as strong as they appear.

It took me a lot of work to see... I realized that this relationship was ending my life. This wasn't living, it was survival. But honestly, I didn't know what to do. I always wondered if he would ever love me or value me.

Towards the end of our relationship I thought whether it was worth praying for him. *Before I continue, I want to make something very clear about prayer. If you were to ask me what got me through this whole ordeal, my answer would be* ***PRAYER and BEING in the PRESENCE OF GOD.*** *But because I didn't see a change for many, many years, I questioned it.* The Bible says, God can do anything, faith moves mountains, why couldn't God change him? I was praying for this. *I was crying out to God about this.* Why didn't God listen to me? What if God was asking me to stay with him to save him?

I knew without a shadow of a doubt I was a good woman. He didn't make me feel that way, but I knew it. I believed in God then and still believe in God now, but I felt trapped being in this abusive relationship for 33 years. How long was I going to support this?

I lived in anguish and in fear. The worst part of it was the obligation I had to the public and church to keep my status as a Pastors wife and show the image that everything was okay. I couldn't share my feelings with anyone. Who could I trust? I had no friends.

People would tell me how beautiful they saw our marriage and family. They always commented on how cute we looked as a couple.

I didn't live in peace, although I was a peace-maker. I was under his control and had no confidence in myself.

To be real, the pain I felt became my comfort zone."

CHAPTER 9

ANCHOR OF HER SOUL

The Heroes in Battle Always Come Back Wounded…

Only God Helped Her Through it…

Lumi always asked herself, how is it possible that I've had the ability to live in an atmosphere of complete abuse; physical, emotional, psychological and verbal abuse. She explained the severity of her day to day living.

One day Lumi wanted to go visit a widowed young lady with her husband but he argued that he was heading somewhere else. She felt he was lying to her, so she got dressed and went on her own. When she arrived, her husband was already there with the woman. It was clear he didn't want her to go with him. Lumi's heart was broken in pieces.

When they both arrived back home, he locked her in the room and started screaming at her, questioning her actions. Lumi asked him why he would do that and speak to her in that manner. His response was, "I am the Pastor and I don't have to give you any explanations."

Her Dialogue with her Father…

That very evening Lumi cried out to the Lord as she did every night for years to pour her heart out to her Heavenly Father. She felt the abuse, the narcissism, the religiosity, the lack of love and consideration. While kneeling in her private prayer room, she would ask God why she was going through this. She would pour out her feelings to God. She felt mistreated, humiliated, rejected, alone, lonely, unaccepted, unloved, and unappreciated. She truly couldn't understand how she could move on another day but, the strength of the Lord and her love for her children gave her enough power to live to the next day.

The Anchor of Her Soul...

You know, that very evening in the mist of that pain and loneliness, the prayer turned into an anchor of her soul. All the time Lumi felt sad and all those feeling of abuse creeped up on her, she would enter God's presence and would feel his counsel and peace in the mist of the storm she was going through. She would get up every day with strength to continue moving forward. She focused her energy on her children. She didn't want to get a divorce. The "D" word was not in her vocabulary. She didn't want her children to suffer what she suffered with her parent's divorce. Although, her husband would even flirt with other women in front of her, she would turn her blind eye and focus on her children and her relationship with God.

When her son, Joey was thrown out of the house, she would park in front of the building he was staying in and pray for him daily. She would cry out to the Lord to protect her son. Her prayer was the same for all four children, Joey, Jay, Janna & Jina.

She Suffered in Silence...

She loved God. She loved the ministry. She loved to serve. Not all pastors' wives are called to ministry and that's okay. However, Lumi was also called to the ministry as well as her husband. They were hand in hand in the calling. She wasn't a woman to sit down and watch. She got down and dirty in the ministry and did all her husband did, if not more. She was immersed in the works of the Lord and the details of the growth of church. She preached, taught, she ran Sunday School and ran the bake sales when she had too.

Lumi saw they had a good thing together if only her husband was faithful and whole in Christ. She would pray and beg God to please change him. She prayed he would have a true encounter with God. Lumi truly believed he was a good man. Her husband served and changed many people's lives. God used him to rebuild families, churches, heal the sick, perform miracles in Jesus's name, and help anyone in need. He took care of the missionary. They both gave them shelter in their home. They provided food for the missionaries from their own pantry and clothing from their own closets, and children's closets. However, those same principles didn't apply to his immediate family.

Lumi begged her husband to go to marriage counseling. She was willing to change to make this work. She would do whatever it took, but he never wanted too. He felt he didn't need counseling; she was the one that had to change. His pride didn't let him look for help. Lumi never spoke about him to anyone, not even her children.

Many times, the victims of abuse are so embarrassed, are in denial, and become desensitize to the abuse, that they feel there's no way out. Resulting in continued abuse in the relationships. Getting out of denial and realizing the truth will set you free and your inner healing will begin.

My God…

Many times, Lumi went to church destroyed inside but with a smile on her face. She felt she was a clown. She was hand in hand with her husband, preaching and teaching and present in every service. They seemed to have the perfect marriage in everyone's eyes. They had a powerful ministry that everyone talked about. He was a leader of authority and power, but little did they know what was happening.

It was a vicious cycle that Lumi hoped would stop one day. It was one night when she prayed to the Lord and He told her to look at her husband's wallet. She got up and obeyed. When she opened it, there was three pictures of three different women. God made her understand, "this is why your marriage won't be restored."

One thing I know is that the precious power and love of God can cover you in the mist of the abuse. Narcissism and religiosity cannot interfere with the Love of God.

It Does Get Better…

In a little under a year, Lumi got herself together and decided she could not be away from her best friend, her God, her Creator. She looked at herself in the mirror and made a decision she would move on. She knew God had nothing to do with her husband's decisions. She would not blame God for anything, but praise Him through the situation. She learned about a person's free will and understood, the decision of change had to come from her husband, not God. She learned that if God could love her more than she loved her children, as the Bible says in John 3:16, she could look fear in the face, get up from her self-pity, her sorrow, her pain, her emptiness and anguish and move on. Through a series of events, Lumi was led to attend a church in the The Bronx, called, "Thessalonica Christian Church."

Lumi's healing began…

Remember the doctor who told Lumi she would end up in a psychiatric ward if she didn't get on medication right away? Well, she proved the doctor wrong. She knew deep inside and through her constant prayer and reading the Bible that the God she served would heal her from all the pain and suffering she went through for 33+ years.

She began to educate herself on inner healing and more importantly began to teach it in Sunday School. She learned that through her selfless act of helping others healing would begin. She let go of any pride, shame and embarrassment the abuse caused her and started focusing on other abused people.

Pastor, Rev. David Serrano, was used immensely by God to help her heal and restore through his teachings and education.

Because her restoration and inner healing was such an impact in the church, the pastor found it appropriate to start a class in Sunday School on Inner Healing. She started with a small class of 10-15 students. In a year or so had over 300 students (men and women) attending her class on inner healing. She taught the class herself for about five to six years.

What is inner healing?

Inner healing or healing of the soul is the process in which you are liberated from bondages that impede you from enjoying every day of your life. It is past hurts and abuse that haunt us in a way that don't allow us to live life to its fullness. It is to have a new life with God and a true realization of who you are in Him.

Isaiah 53:4-6, 11 New International Version (NIV)

4 Surely, he took up our pain and bore our suffering, yet we considered him punished by God, stricken by him, and afflicted.

5 But he was pierced for our transgressions, he was crushed for our iniquities the punishment that brought us peace was on him, and by his wounds we are healed.

6 We all, like sheep, have gone astray, each of us has turned to our own way; and the Lord has laid on him the iniquity of us all.

11 After he has suffered, he will see the light of life and be satisfied; by his knowledge my righteous servant will justify many, and he will bear their iniquities.

What does inner healing consist of?

Inner healing is related to the past of the individual. In your emotional life, there is no time nor space in what has affected you. Your pain will come back to attack your present and your future.

We just need to take hold of the promises of God to be healed.

What are some promises of God amongst many?

- The Lord will fight for you…Exodus 14:14
- Honor your Father & your Mother… Exodus 20:12
- He gives strength to the weary and increases power of the weak Isaiah 40:29
- …but those who hope in the Lord will renew their strength Isaiah 40:31
- So do not fear, for I am with you; do not be dismayed, for I am your God. I will strengthen you and help you; I will uphold you with my righteous right hand. Isaiah 41:10
- If any of you lacks wisdom, you should ask God, who gives generously to all without finding fault, and it will be given to you. James 1:5
- The LORD himself goes before you and will be with you; he will never leave you nor forsake you. Do not be afraid; do not be discouraged. Deuteronomy 31:8
- For I know the plans I have for you," declares the LORD, "plans to prosper you and not to harm you, plans to give you hope and a future. Jeremiah 29:11
- So if the Son sets you free, you will be free indeed. John 8:36
- Therefore, I tell you, whatever you ask for in prayer, believe that you have received it, and it will be yours. Mark 11:24
- … Be strong and courageous. Do not be afraid; do not be discouraged, for the LORD your God will be with you wherever you go." Joshua 1:9
- And my God will meet all your needs according to the riches of his glory in Christ Jesus. Philippians 4:19

We need to understand the effects that painful experiences and traumas have in our lives.

We are the product of all the experiences we go through. Our past experiences determine our relationships in the present. The hurts in our past, distorts what we perceive in the present, to the point that we react to a simple problem with violence, depression etc. We can conclude, that we are not responding normally to certain situations because we have bondages in our lives.

How does hurt come and what are the most common ways it does?

The basic emotional needs of a man are satisfied through love and communication. Rejection provokes man not to receive love, assurance, and acceptance. Rejection is a deep wound that causes destruction to an individual.

Proverbs 28:13-14 New International Version (NIV)

[13] Whoever conceals their sins does not prosper, but the one who confesses and renounces them finds mercy.

[14] Blessed is the one who always trembles before God, but whoever hardens their heart falls into trouble.

It is very important to recognize what you've never recognized, accept what you've never accepted and confess what you've never confessed.

Confession Frees the Soul

She felt free to be herself for the very first time in her life. The process of healing consisted of realizing her hurt, forgiving and repeating the process until time healed all wounds. It didn't happen one day to another but, one thing Lumi always says,

"The Best Thing You Have Is One Day After Another..."

CHAPTER 10

THE EFFECT ON HER DAUGHTER...

Lumi's children amongst many people suffered this man's abuse and infidelity. Her children carried it with them for some time, each of them shedding the weight in their own time. The blow hit them each differently and while not all her children are ready to share their whole truth... here's my truth.

The Beginning Does Not Define the END...

I grew up in the church and enjoyed it. I was always busy. My parents had me involved in church and in school. As children, my sister and I were involved in the children's ministry and participated in every event. We were in marching bands in elementary school & JHS. My sister played the Clarinet and I played the xylophone and tom, toms. We participated in the Puerto Rican parade and in the Christian parade for a few years in a row. I remember my parents having so much influence in the school, to the extent that the uniform for the girls changed from pants to skirts because we couldn't wear pants for religious reasons. Everywhere we went, my parents had influence.

As a teenager, I was involved in the youth ministries in the church and association of churches we participated in. From the age of 13 years old I worked and made my own money. I went to Fashion Industries in the city of NY, worked in the NY Public Library and was the youngest to start Bible Institute and the youngest to graduate. I was always busy doing something productive. Thanks to my parents who motivated us to work hard and move forward in our lives. I graduated HS in 3½ years and my Bachelor's degree in 3½. This was not on purpose, I just wanted to hurry up and finish because I didn't like school. My mother always told me to be independent. She always said, "Go to school, get a good education so you could get a good job." So, that was what I did.

I was 20 years old now and had just graduated with two bachelor's degrees, one in Psychology and the other in Sociology. I knew this education would serve me well in the church. I remember my graduation being so sad. There were no plans of celebration. My father had just left the house and the divorce was on its way. It was a sad time for the whole family. I was the first from my siblings to graduate from college so I thought at least there would be a happy celebration. I don't blame my mom, it just happened to be one of the worst times of her life, our lives. I went to the graduation ahead by myself. I really didn't have any friends in college. It was school, work then church. There was no time to join any clubs or socialize in the university. I waited for my family attentively, but they got there late and had to sit in the overflow. I have no pictures because my mother's camera got messed up. It couldn't get any worse. I was so hurt and disappointed. We did go eat afterwards but the tension was so high. I ran to church after the graduation and thought for sure someone will be happy for me. But because education wasn't really promoted in the church, everyone just went about their own business.

Shortly after my parents split, my older brother, Joey shared some ugly truth with me. He looked so intensely at me and confessed everything he knew, and he knew everything. He'd known since he was a child. He remembers as far back as 3-4 years old seeing our father with other women. One of his first huge beatings at 3-4 years old was when he confessed to our mother what he had seen. He saw it with his own eyes. This wasn't the first time our father had done this. I couldn't believe it. I was in shock and disbelief.

My father had been with women who were married. Women who served in ministry alongside my mother. Women who came over to our house and shared our food. Women my mother considered friends and daughters. Women I looked up to. Women who were my friends. Women, who I'd share my room with. I felt betrayed by everyone around me.

I continued to serve in the church and started socializing more. I had good friends including guy friends. It was liberating in a sense not to have my father hovering over me anymore. I could be more independent. I felt accomplished. I had my first real job as a counselor after college. I had my own car and I was ready for the world.

I always dated guys in the church who were involved in ministry somehow. But each relationship failed in some way or another. The first guy I dated left me out of guilt of being unfaithful. Thereafter, I dated three pastors' kids. I didn't realize this until speaking about it. All three relationships failed. They were all going through their own struggles. One had gotten sexually abuse by a close family member, the second, had issues with commitment, insecurities and low self-esteem, and the third was going through the trauma of his own parents divorcing. Then, I met the man of my dreams or so I thought.

A Rose for a Rose

He was new to the church and he seemed to come at the perfect time. My sister had gotten with the man of her dreams from church and now it looked like it was my turn to find someone. Or rather, to be found.

He had come from Puerto Rico and was a very talented preacher and very smart. His intelligence was the first thing that drew me to him. He wasn't only educated in the Word of God but educated in the real world too. He wasn't like the other guys I met before in church who didn't value education. He was well-spoken and was charismatic. Every time he preached, I was blown away by his knowledge and how deep he could be. He was also my best friends' cousin which made it comfortable to have a relationship.

We became friends and the more time we spent with each other the more I was falling for him. He was the type that wasn't afraid to talk about his feelings and his passions. He liked sharing his goals and creating new ones with me. I found that to be so attractive when we began dating. He liked talking about our future. He liked talking about getting a house with me one day and having kids and becoming better together. We understood each other on so many levels. The more I think about it, the more I realize, he was the exact opposite of my father in almost every way… or was he?

I was getting the love and affirmation I never got from my father. Was this it? Was he the truly the one? He even got along so well with my sister and her husband. It all fit so well.

However, he would get upset about how much time I was spending at church. He felt that the church was taking advantage of me. He didn't realize church was my life. Although, I had been through disappointments with my father and people in the church, I had my own relationship with God and loved to serve. I was the only young women ordained minister in the church. I was a Sunday School teacher. I counseled young women. I led support groups. I played the drums and was part of the worship team. And if that wasn't enough, I also worked in a creative ministry writing and creating the monthly newsletter, flyers and comic books. After everything I had been through with the church, I didn't want to believe that. I had been hurt enough. But this man was so gentle and kind, I felt he wanted the best for me. So, I started spending more time with him and less at the church.

Listen to the person the first time they tell you who they are…

A part of me wonders if I felt like I was running out of options. None of the guys I already knew were treating me right and I didn't want to wait on who would come along next. My sister got married and I was the only one at the house. My mother did comment she felt he wasn't the one, but she was also wooed by his intelligence and great Bible teachings, so she accepted him. He convinced me to be against church and his family, but I just thought he cared for me so much; he was protecting me. He wanted to go all the way with me before marriage, but I would constantly convince him to wait. It was my honor to give him all of me on our wedding day. He even wanted to have children as he longed to be a daddy. His father had passed away when he was 16. He was a heroin addict and died of AIDS. There were signed and I overlooked them. There's always signs. Pay attention. Nonetheless, I felt I had found my soulmate, so when he proposed, I happily said yes.

We had our dream wedding. It was perfect. The perfect dress, the perfect venue, the perfect bridesmaids, flower girls and the perfect honeymoon. Over 200 guests showed up. Everyone had a blast. Every detail of the wedding was spectacular.

We moved close to my mother's home. I was so happy to be married and be close to my family as well. Nine months later, we discovered I was pregnant, and we were both ecstatic. I knew he was good with kids. Before I got pregnant, we had gone to visit my sister in Florida and got to meet my niece. He loved her instantly and seeing him happily play with a gurgling baby only confirmed to me that when it was our turn, he would be a good dad.

Thereafter, he strongly suggested we move to Arizona to grow our current financial business together and make all our dreams come true. We had started a finance business right before we got married and it was growing. I was so mixed up and in love I didn't even consider my mother in the situation. My mother had gotten a divorce with my father not too long ago. My sister had gotten married and moved to Florida and now I was leaving her with an empty nest. I was the last one my mother was keeping it together for. I was all she had during her darkest hour. I didn't know that while I was experiencing the happiest moments of my life, my mother's life was breaking down at home. She was really alone this time.

I called my mother with the exciting news not knowing that although this added happiness to my life, it was like rock thrown to hers. But she didn't let me know she was aching on the inside. She let me make my own choices and let me live my life the way I wanted to live it. She didn't want to hold me back. As I was moving on with my life my mother was going through her own healing journey and while she anchored me for many years, this was a journey my mother had to make alone.

My mother remembers being so depressed but making sure she didn't let me know how she felt as she didn't want me to feel bad leaving. Her friend Gladys was her anchor through those tough times. She thanks her for that.

A month passes as we move to Arizona and settle into our new home. We were so in tune with each other. I would think something, and he would say it the next second. I would feel cold for a second and he would be wrapping me in a blanket the next second. It was to the point where it was almost scary and sometimes annoying. He took good care of me, making sure I had everything I needed, always asking how I was doing and pouring me with attention. A month passes in Arizona and then he turns on me.

To me it seemed to happen overnight.

We would go to conferences together and business meetings. We did everything together to make this business happen. We were working together on this. And then one day, he just stopped. He didn't want to attend the conferences and go to meetings and make phone calls. I began doing it all myself. I was the one working to support us.

Suddenly, he didn't want to cuddle with me anymore and he seemed to care about me out of obligation and not love. His interactions weren't the same anymore.

We went to a church who was looking for a Spanish speaking pastor. We were offered the position. It was a big AG church of over 5,000 members and they loved us. We believed it was God sent but he did nothing to follow up.

Our apartment was a two bedroom and he began spending a lot of time in the other room on the computer. I confronted him about it eventually. "Are you seeing another woman? Why are you being so cold with me?" And he turned to me and simply said "God left him."

CHAPTER 11

PAIN IS AN INDICATION THAT SOMETHING MUST CHANGE…

"No, he can get through this."
"No, this is who I am."
"Let's go to therapy."

"God left me," he said. I was so confused. I knew my God would not leave anyone. I kept on asking him and nagging him to tell me what was going on. He wasn't making any sense. I knew a man that analyzed the word of God. He was the preachers of preachers. I screamed and asked, "What are you talking about?"

Stop trying to change and control people, the only thing you can control is how you react to your situation.

I was 2 months pregnant and my husband confesses to me, *he's gay.* "What?" I told him. I was so confused. It came completely out of the blue. "What are you talking about?" I told him crying. "We are married, how could you be gay?" I was perturbed. I felt deceived and angry. At first, I didn't believe him. I thought he was going through a phase because I was pregnant and it was bringing him a lot of confused feelings. I paced back and forth trying to make sense of the situation. Trying to fix it. But he would come back to telling me, "I'm gay." "How could he do this to me?" I was thinking. "I'm about to give birth to your child." "Didn't he know who he was before he married me?" I felt alone, disoriented but mostly deceived. I thought, "Isn't this the same guy who wanted a baby before we were married. Now he is having one and he is leaving me?" This made no sense to me. I thought we had a great marriage and a great sex life. I screamed and pleaded to him to explain to me what was happening. I was a church girl. I didn't know anything about this lifestyle. If there were signed, I would have not picked up on that. He was very manly in my eyes and everyone's eyes that I knew. I screamed, "What are you talking about, now you're gay. What?"

My womanhood was shaken. "Did I turn him gay?" I asked herself. I quickly put on my social work hat and began to research men who live on the downlow. It was then I knew without a shadow of a doubt, it wasn't me. Making me feel more deceived and angrier and completely alone. "Who could I share this with?" I couldn't tell my mom. I didn't want to hurt her. I thought somehow this situation would be fixed before I would have to tell her. I couldn't tell my family; they would literally hurt him. I found the courage to tell my best friend. She was there for me. She tried helping me by directing me to a church who dealt with these situations. The church reached out to me telling me, "things won't change unless he wants too." The problem was he didn't want to change. He felt he was born this way.

Why marry me then? Did he marry me to portray that he was straight and not gay? Did he love me? Was the preaching just a façade? So many questions and so little answers.

I began to question God. "haven't I prayed to you Lord, since before my teenage years to please do not allow me to marry the wrong person? What's going on?" I would cry out to God to please fix this, but it was getting worse and worse. My whole world as I knew it was wiped right under my feet.

My emotions were all over the place. One day I would wake up wanting to work it out and the other I would wake up angry wanting to hurt him. One day I wanted to hug him and say all will be alright and the next I wanted to throw him out of the house. One day I would want to have a deep conversation with him and the next day I wanted to run away from the house. My feelings were up and down every day. My belly was growing, and I had to make a mental decision to stop the emotional madness. I had self-improved enough to know my mind needed to be right for my emotions to follow. I had read the word of God enough to know there had to be a way out. The difficulty was trying to control my emotions while pregnant. I had no one I felt comfortable enough to speak too. I had recently moved to another state where I had no friends.

For a very short period, I contemplated getting rid of my fetus but quickly came back to my senses and decided to live for my baby. Also, the financial chaos we were going through, kept me busy. He didn't only tell me he was gay, he also stopped providing for me, for us. He stopped working and wasn't trying to provide. His life was sleep and chatting on the computer. I started losing everything. I didn't have a job and we were out of money. No one would hire me because I was starting to show. I had to figure out what to do because I had to take care of this baby that was on its way. I forced him to go to christian counseling with hopes they could figure this out, but the counselor said I had to accept the reality that he was born this way.

I didn't understand. I was all alone. I had no friends, no neighbors I could confide in, no acquaintances, no church family, absolutely nobody. "Was this what life had for me? I kept my purity for my husband, for this? I listened to my parents, for this? I gave my all to the church, for this?" I had a feast in my self-pity every day. I cried myself to sleep every single day, but every day I spoke to myself that all would work out. I had to survive for my baby. Little did I know that God was saving me from a horrible future if I had stayed.

"Be uncomfortable today so you can claim your greatness tomorrow"

I didn't know at the time, but he was on the internet all the time looking at other men and chatting with them. I was so innocent hoping for the best so much that I even allowed him to go away on a weekend to Las Vegas with a guy he met on the internet. He said it was just "friends." I was about 5-6 months pregnant. He left for a whole weekend, which seemed like eternity to me. I was in a strange state, all alone. Little did I know God was saving me from misery. Saving me from decease. Saving me from depression. Saving me from extreme anxiety. God was giving me a way out. He was listening to my prayers in my early years about who I would marry.

I was broke but not POOR…

We were so broke, I had made appointments to social services to see if they could help. The place we lived in placed notices of eviction every month on our door. I went to food pantries. I got on welfare, WIC and Medicaid. I was doing everything I could to survive while he stayed home sleeping and on the computer. I ran up my mother's credit card and emptied out all our bank accounts. We literally had no food in our fridge at times and I would somehow fall into favor through God and get food. Somehow, even though our bank accounts were at zero, I would find ways to keep us alive. In Arizona the water from the tap wasn't safe to drink. We had to get water from a filter. It was 25 cents a gallon of drinkable water. We didn't even have that.

I would carry a big purse to my doctors' appointments so I could steal toilet paper from the bathroom. I would return the WIC milk in exchange for store credit, to get food. The things I did to survive were real. I needed to feed my baby. I look on those times now and I'm truly amazed how God carried us through it. We were broker than broke. But through it all God was showing me His grace. He was carrying me through it. I had the footprint of Jesus in my heart. I knew who I was in Christ and knew somehow I would figure it out. I always thought, "It will all work out somehow." "I have a degree, I will get us back on our feet. I'm broke now but it's only temporary." I learned these things in church. I listened to the word of God. God was equipping me with strength because I was obedient to my parents and I genuinely loved God. Although, I couldn't articulate my feelings or actions at the time, the residue of my commitment to God came into play in my darkest times.

God's Grace and Favor is not irrevocable...

I remember going to social services for help to find out there wasn't any money to help us. But God grace and favor was so strong on me that the workers would bless me with their personal money. I remember one social worker reaching into her purse and handing me a twenty-dollar bill. At that time, it was like being handed a gold mine. She made me promise I wouldn't say anything because she would get in trouble for doing this, but the social worker felt so compelled she had to do it. I thankfully accepted the cash and walked out of there thanking God. Right when I thought we would starve I would get handed a little something to get us through the next day.

Even though I was seeing miracles like this happen to me, I was still struggling with my relationship with God. It was a daily mental struggle. I would thank God for providing but then questioned Him for our broken marriage. A lot of mixed emotions.

I remember calling my mother to ask if she could send me food without detailing our financial status. She sent us 'pasteles', a very well-known Puerto Rican dish. I was so hungry that I ate so many too fast, I ended up throwing them up. The pantry food just wasn't enough.

One day on my usual routine to go to the stores to return items in exchange for food, I got stuck in my car. The doors wouldn't open. It was at least 110 degrees and I thought for sure I would die since I didn't have any air conditioner in the car and the windows were rolled up. I saw my life flash by my eyes. If that wasn't enough, a fire truck passed right by the car and I couldn't get their attention to help me. God finally made me realized I could open the door manually and ran out of the car. From then on, I began to have episodes of panic, anxiety, fear and claustrophobia just like my mother.

There were no finances coming into the house. He claimed he couldn't work. He was too depressed. He would say he couldn't breathe. He needed to go out to the gay bars every night and needed to be around people like him. He needed to party at night to survive. He wasn't alive until he was out surrounded by his crowd. I couldn't understand that. I could understand the depression but, allowing me and his baby to starve was unacceptable. Didn't he realize he had a baby on its way and a very pregnant wife who needed nurturing and care? But the narcissist does not see that. They see their needs and wants, above all.

I was living for my baby inside me. I wanted to have her. "He'll come around," I thought. I prayed for him. I did exactly what my mother did for my father. I prayed for him to change. I thought, "He's going to change, he's going to get better." After seeing what my mother went through, I prayed that I would marry the right guy. I wanted to have a better relationship than my parents.

I was maybe 5-6 months pregnant when my mother started calling me telling me she was having nightmares about me. She was sensing something was wrong with me. She was worried about me. She knew nothing of what was going on. "Mommy, there's nothing going on. Relax."

A relief in the mist of the storm…

My mother told me to go to NY to throw me a surprise baby shower. God was giving me some relief. I was able to see all my friends and church family. They celebrated my new bundle of joy to come. But while I smiled and laughed, my heart was broken. My husband was strongly encouraging me to stay in NY and not return. But I didn't listen. "How could I give birth without the father of my child being present." I wasn't even taking my feelings into account. It was always about him. He continued to repeat to me to stay in NY and not return to Arizona, but I didn't listen. I couldn't do it.

The stress of the situation landed me in the hospital in NY. I started bleeding and my mother had to rush me to the hospital. I had a little wakeup call that it wasn't about him, it was about my baby who was growing inside of me. I refocused and made the decision again to take care of myself and my baby. The hospital hydrated me and sent me home.

While in NY, I attended my church to worship with my mother and spend time with my friends. Little did I know God had another relief and comfort for my soul there. The preacher that night was talking about prosperity and having more than enough. Considering my broke situation, I embraced the word closed to my heart. But then the preacher said, "to get to the level God wants you to be in, you need to give Him all you have." The only thing I had was a $100.00 bill in my pocket, which was given to me as a baby shower gift. "Oh no," I said, "He is not talking to me." I battled and battled inside. I knew I was being tested. Was I going to listen? I knew I had to give it all because I was meant to be prosperous. I've always the calling of giving over my life. I couldn't hold my destiny any longer and past to the front and gave that crispy $100.00 bill. Wow, what a peace I felt. I knew I had done the right thing. Thank God I listened. You'll find out later why.

I went to church before I was married searching for answers. I was prophesied by the pastor's wife that my marriage was of God. This was it, the confirmation I needed. I thought this was right. Looking back on it, I honestly don't think I was wrong. God gave me to him so he wouldn't have any excuse about being restored or about being complete.

How could God leave you when he gave you such a good woman, and about to have your first born? This was his chance. He was dealt the right cards. It was his move. I was willing to stay. I wanted to work it out. He had a choice to make. And even if I am wrong about it all, I still believe this was meant to happen.

Without him I wouldn't have my first born. If it was all just to have her…then it was all worth it.

She Needed to be Born…

Just when I thought I couldn't do it anymore, his aunt from NY, moved in with us. Titi Aida, three children and granddaughter moved to Arizona to start their lives over. They were God sent. God used her as the perfect distraction. She brought a joy that wasn't there. She knew what was going on and was as confused as me, but she brought a sense of peace to the house. She took care of us, played games with us, bought food, brought me to my doctor's appointments and kept me company. She was there for me. She was there for us. I appreciate every little thing she did, till this day.

Not too long after, they got their own place. Thank God she remained a part of our lives.

The baby was ready to come. Although her due date was in November, I gave birth a month and a half earlier. The doctors thought the baby would be pre-mature, but instead she was pre-term. The doctors had determined my due date incorrectly.

On October 12th before going to bed, I go to the bathroom as usual but this time I couldn't stop going. I had no pain, so I didn't think much of it. When I mention it to my husband, he realized my water had broken. Although I wanted a natural water birth and my room was ready for the delivery, I needed medical attention.

For a short moment I forgot the reality of our broken marriage. I was so happy that he was concerned about me and I was feeling loved again. He grabbed me gently and drove me to the hospital right away with the luggage he had prepared for me. His constant worry about me made me feel everything was going to be okay with us. I was sure this was what he needed to change.

He drove me to the hospital and carefully placed me on a wheel chair to bring me in. Our aunt was waiting for us there. I heard him talking to the nurses saying, "my wife and my child." It was music to my ears. I said to myself, "I'm his wife again, we are a family, we will leave from the hospital as a family." I had brought pictures of us in an album and sat it next to the bed to see "My Family." All the nurses commented on his care for me and the beautiful pictures. It was going to be okay, I thought. "We are a family again."

Although I was disappointed that my mother wasn't there, the feeling that I was getting my husband back, made me feel complete. He was excited about the heartbeat. He was joking around with us and I thought, "this is it." The baby being born will change him. She thought, "This is just a phase."

Then, reality hit me. He left to change clothing and came back speaking about a friend of his. I got so angry and realized nothing had changed. I thought, "I'm in full blown labor pains and here he is talking about some friend that could be someone he is with." I wanted to hurt him, but I had to refocus. I was in labor pains and was not dilating. I was in too much stress. The nurses didn't know what was going on but were advising me to relax. God knows I was trying to. They concluded to give me an epidural after 36 hours of labor pain. I thought "wow, they couldn't suggest that earlier?" I was in so much pain, I thought she was going to die. 36 hours of full blown labor pains is no joke. My body relaxed and 48 hours later, I gave birth to the most beautiful baby girl on October 14th, 2001.

Oh, what a joy it was. I looked at a 5 pound and 18-ounce baby girl, and knew the pain was all worth it. I looked at me straight in my eyes validating I was her mom. She rested on my chest and it was there I realized how much my mom loved me. You can't explain the love until you experience motherhood yourself. My first baby girl made me a mom. She gave me strength to move on. She was perfect.

Maybe he'll change once the baby is born. ...

My baby was so tiny and precious, but I could hardly enjoy it all because I was stressed about my husband getting his act together so we could raise our daughter together. Just like we use to talk about, what seemed like ages ago. And now that we finally were parents, he was more concerned with going out at night and trying to figure himself out than our baby.

My mother, sister and brother-in-law came to visit us in Arizona to see the baby. They all knew something was off but I wouldn't share the truth. I was always trying to protect him. My husband self-centeredness got so bad that my mother had to pull him to the side and question his behavior. Everything was about his well-being and not the well-being of the baby and of me. I was devastated to have to side with my husband knowing my mother was right, but that was what I was taught.

I quickly got a job as a social worker, when our baby girl was 2-3 weeks old. I found the strength to get back on my feet because of her. I was educated. God had given me health and

I was not going to depend on the government when I could work. I started working and providing for the home while he was still depressed. I would get up in the morning; breast feed, get the baby dressed, take her to Titi Aida's house, go to work, pump on my lunch hour in the bathroom, run back to pick her up, breast feed her again and go back home. Every night I would get an upset stomach around 8:30 pm as that was the time he would start getting dressed to go to the clubs. He was still going out and not working. He kept saying he couldn't live without going out at night. He had the energy to get dressed up every single night to go out but not a job to support his family. I couldn't understand.

I finally got so fed up with him one day while he stayed up all night on the computer. I stood up and said, "I can't do this anymore." I picked up the baby, which was 2 months old, and left the house. I got in my car and by the time I drove around the corner the baby started screaming. I suddenly realized I had left all her things behind. What was I doing? The baby needed clothes, baby food, and diapers. I couldn't just drive off into the night without those things. I went back to the apartment a little flustered. I didn't even think of breastfeeding. Something compelled me to drive back home.

It Gets Worse Before It Gets Better…

He was talking very strangely when I returned. I remember him saying something about the sky being purple. I sat down to get a bottle for the baby, and he walked out of the room looking dazed. I raised my eye brows at him not sure what was going on when he suddenly passed out with a hard *thud*. "What did you do?" I screamed and ran to him. Not knowing what to do, I raced to the phone and called 911 as he was mumbling to me that he couldn't live. I paced around the house in a panic as the phone rang. There was a ton of pills in the bathroom. I couldn't focus on anything. I didn't understand.

"911 what's your emergency?"

"My husband, he fell down! I think he tried to kill himself!" I went back to him and grabbed him.

Everything seemed to happen so fast yet so slow. I remember some moment so vividly and yet other have completely escaped my memory. Like during this entire altercation, I can see myself holding him in my arms. I can see him looking up at me as I'm asking him why he would do this? how could he do this? All he said was that he was so sorry and that he loved me. And for the life of me, I can't remember where the baby was. Was she crying? She must have been, but I can't hear her voice in the background. It's just the banging of the door getting kicked in as a couple of firemen storm in and pried me off my husband.

They searched the house and started yelling "How could you do this? You have a wife and child?" Everything was spinning. One of the firemen told me, if they would have arrived a minute later, he would have died. I called my aunt to let her know what was going on. I rushed to grab my keys as he was being carried off. I couldn't find my keys for a moment. I was frantic. I dropped off the baby at my aunt's house and went to the hospital. When I arrived, they refused to let me see my husband. They told me, I would make it worse for him. I didn't understand. I was his wife. How could I make things worse for him when I was there to help him? Did he say something about me that's making them keep us apart?

He stayed in the hospital for nearly two weeks. I went to work the very next day and told my manager the situation. He understood the lifestyle. God works in mysterious ways. He said "Take all the time you need. We'll figure it out."

Once he came back home, I was ready to make things work with him again. I tried to spend more time with him. I tried to take him out to the movies, go shopping or out to eat. Now that I had the money for it, I wanted to spoil him. In a way, I was trying to bribe him into being with me, but off course, it didn't last.

The baby was ten months when I remember, he didn't come home until the next morning. I knew exactly what he had done. It was time for me to leave. He came in the house that morning saying he wanted to show off his daughter to his partner and I completely refused. My heart was broken; I knew I had to leave.

I called my sister and told her I was going through some money troubles and she offered me an opportunity to live with her until we could get thing figured out. I didn't reveal everything that was going on but I'm sure my sister knew it wasn't just about the money. Before I left, I asked my manager if I still would have a job there in case I came back. My manager said yes. There was still a part of me that was hoping we could find a way to each other again. I was open to the possibility that there was a chance and maybe if I left for a while, he would see that too.

I went to Florida. My brother-in-law got me a job as a teacher. I worked and spent my spare time taking care of my niece, nephew my baby and working out. About a month later he calls me saying "I've changed." I willingly picked up all my belongings and the baby and went back to him expecting us to start right back where we left off before everything went south in our relationship. The baby's 1st birthday was approaching, and I wanted to celebrate together as a family. I wanted him to be a father; apparently more than he did.

When I arrived to our apartment, I saw it was decorated with all these pro-gay posters and I turned to him and say, "You lied to me." He had not changed at all. If anything, he was worse than when I had left. We celebrated the baby's 1st birthday together as planned and I worked for a while at my old job in Arizona until finally she knew I couldn't stay any longer and headed back to my sister's house.

Here I am sleeping on the couch at her sister's house while sending money to my husband in Arizona. He manipulated me in so many ways. He would tell me we were still married, and I needed to take care of him. He was still refusing to get a job. He was still my husband and I still loved him.

At this point I couldn't hide what was going on any longer. I told my sister and her husband what was really going on and we all cried together. I stayed in Florida for a little less than a year. I constantly did things to keep busy, to keep my mind off my failed relationship. But, if that wasn't enough, I had overstayed my welcome at my sister's house and needed to move out. I left on a rainy night to stay with a co-worker while I was looking for a place to stay. Before I could find a place to live, my mother came to get me. She came to visit me on Thanksgiving and unexpectantly said, "You're coming with me."

So, I returned to NY with my mother by my side.

Chapter 12

ANGER WILL TERMINATE THE DESTINY GOD HAS FOR YOU…

I was angry.

I had been the best I could be. The best wife I could be and in the end my marriage couldn't be restored. I prayed hard for something to turn around and nothing did. We spoke for hours as I questioned him about the situation. As a social worker at heart, I started to ask him more profound questions about his childhood. In one of those conversations, he confessed to me being sexually abused as a child by a man. It seemed to simple to me to see this was why he was having issues with his sexuality. I prayed he would be healed and understand he wasn't born this way. The reality is that studies show, sexual abuse does cause brain injury in minors, causing trauma and the ability to identify and develop emotional maturity. The American Nurse Official Journal, has an article on "Long-term health outcomes of Childhood sexual abuse," detailing some of the effects. When a child is sexually abused, it confuses their thought process. I personally saw this being very common in victims who had issues with drug abuse, alcoholism, promiscuity and sexual dysfunction.

At this point, it wasn't even about restoring my marriage, it was about raising our daughter. He didn't support our baby financially, and it was always inconvenient for him to see her. I was so desperate for him to be a part of our child's life that I would even pay him to come see her. If he wanted eat, I would get the food. If he needed a ride, I would provide it. He needed money, I gave it to him. Since he moved around, I drove where ever he was so he can see her. But even that didn't keep him committed.

I had been the best Christian girl for so long and I was played. I needed to blow off steam. I thought I needed to let my hair down and forget my troubles. I started clubbing with friends from church and going out with men. I was desperately looking for love and satisfaction in all the wrong places. But I needed a distraction or a solution of some kind.

Unfortunately, the solution I was looking for was not in the clubs nor with men, but I didn't care. I wanted to have fun. I was an adult. I could do what I wanted. I didn't have to listen to my mother anymore. I had a child. I was good. Big mistake!

I was blinded by the temporary happiness of this world and confused love with sex. I tired having serious relationships but the men from the world where not like the men I dated in church. They were expecting more without any real commitments. Since I was surrounding myself with likeminded people, it became normal to date this way. I had destructive relationships and didn't realize it until months later. I started to casually date but didn't know how too.

I remember dating a car salesman. We spoke on the phone for months to finally meet and go out on a real date. I was excited to be courted by this tall, blue eyes, professional man who seemed to be a gentleman. We met in a close by mall to go out to dinner. He seemed happy to see me but approached me with a forceful kiss. When I backed up, he smiled and said," come on you know we've been waiting for this." However, I truly wanted to keep it pure. Have diner, a good conversation and maybe a goodnight kiss. He smiled and kissed me anyway. I knew something was off but was giving him the benefit of the doubt. He then sat in the back of the car claiming he wanted to chat but before I could even say "no" or push him away, I became a victim of date rape. It happened so fast. I was dazed and confused. As a way of escape I just claimed I had a severe headache and went home. I never saw him or heard from him again.

Although, it is never the victim's fault when something like this happens, I felt worthless and brushed it off as if somehow, I deserved it or it wasn't a big deal. At this point I had over stayed my visit at my sister's house, so I had to move out. I was all alone staying with a co-worker in Florida. My friend loved this guy, so I felt safe dating him. What a mistake!

I continued to date to find out another guy I was dating was married, so that didn't last. I knew better. As I moved back to NY nothing changed. I alway took care of my responsibilities with my baby but once a week while my baby slept, I would go party with my church friends.

One night while in a club with my sister-in-law, I met this charming guy. We exchanged numbers and started to date. He seemed to come from a good family. He had a career and seemed to have a good head on his shoulders. He always courted me and showed me off to his friends. He introduced me to his parents and shared his goals with me. However, I never did the same. He didn't know my daughter or my family. I was very caution in letting anyone in. I wanted to wait to see if this was real.

Almost a year into our relationship, I thought I had gotten pregnant. When I told him, he denied it. I was in awe. "What? I told him," how could those words come out of your mouth." He was scared and didn't know what to do. I reflected on my life and couldn't believe how low I had gone. I had given him the most intimate parts of myself and he was denying our relationship. I felt worthless. I felt dirty. The girl I once knew, meant nothing to the men I was meeting. The doctor said I was days pregnant and there was no heartbeat, so I took a morning after pill and terminated the pregnancy. I was a walking zombie. Trying to find love in all the wrong places.

It got to the point that I felt this was my life. My expectations were low. My self-esteem and self-image were attacked. I had temporary fun with my friends but deep inside I knew this life would end up in destruction. I felt empty, alone and depressed. I would choose the worse day in my church life a million times over, before choosing the life I was living, but I felt there was no hope for me. I felt disgusted of myself but stayed busy not to think about it. I just kept going. I eventually stayed by herself taking care of my baby.

I kept in contact with my daughter's father. He would tell me things that I'm was sure were only traps to get me to come back and take care of him. He even suggested a way that we could still be together. He had seen an episode of Oprah where this lifestyles family was exactly what he thought we needed for us to work. We would just live as life partners. We would still be married and live in the same home, we could have a couple of more kids together and raise them. But I also had to accept him for who he was and allow him to have men on the side. He said, "no one would have to know what was going down." It could just be our thing. Our own way of living that would satisfy everyone. Except, that wouldn't satisfy me. I knew the kind of relationship I wanted and deserved. That was the final straw. I knew it was totally over between us then and there was no going back once we signed those papers.

I focused on getting back on my feet. I couldn't find a job. I wasn't getting any child support. I had no form of income coming in. I was carrying over $50K in debt from Arizona. My car was being reprocessed. I was desperate. My brother, Joey had given me his name to get the car. I appreciated him so much that I didn't want to mess up his credit. I needed money fast.

He found a job and I thought for sure he would start helping me, but he always had excuses why he couldn't. I believe he gave me money once or twice, but that was it. The last time I asked him to help, he sadly told me he got molested and now he had a terminal illness like his dad. I didn't know what to say. I cried and pray he would run back to God. Thereafter, he told me he couldn't help me anymore. He felt he no longer could work because of his health.

My mother pushed me to get a divorce and get full custody. I was willing to give him split custody but he didn't want to sign for a divorce. He wanted me to take care of him as I had that responsibility as his wife. He told me the same thing my father told my mother, divorce is not of God. Right! But being with men and staying married is? I finally went through with the divorce. I was so hurt and devastated by the whole situation that I cut myself off from God and the church.

The day I had to go to court for the divorce I felt so alone. I went by herself. I thought he would show up, but he didn't. I felt like a failure. Although I knew I had done everything in my power to make it work, I still felt like a loser. "Here I am going through a divorce like my mother," I thought. "All that church and none of it worked."

What a lie from the devil. God was saving me from misery all along, I just couldn't see it.

Open your eyes and see the Greatness of God all around you.

Anchor of My Soul

There was a time where my mother contemplated whether she would have me or not. In the end I knew I was meant to live.

Now that I was back under my mother's roof, we began spending a lot of time together. Even though for a while I was partying and not putting God first in my life, my mother was still there for me. It was like old times in a way. Food was cooked, clothes was cleaned, I had someone to talk too, and someone to hold me when I needed to be held. Someone to watch out for me.

I had been so angry for so long that I didn't even realize it was all meant to make me the woman I am today. We can never grow and become the person God has created us to be if we're not constantly learning and growing. Just like a flower; if we're not growing, we're dying. We need to be tested and stretched to find out who we're all about. Part of growth is going through sufferings and struggles. The Bible talks about going through struggles in this world as part of experiences we go through in life to become better.

Romans 5:3-6 New International Version (NIV) 5 [3] **...** but we also glory in our sufferings, because we know that suffering produces perseverance; [4] perseverance, character; and character, hope. [5] And hope does not put us to shame, because God's love has been poured out into our hearts through the Holy Spirit, who has been given to us.

When we are confronted with tribulation, anguish, persecution, hunger, nakedness, and danger, it is tempting to think that God has abandoned us, and He doesn't love us. But I share from personal experience and from the facts I lived, that the perfect love of God was there and had a plan in whatever situation I was facing. The true reality of Jesus's sacrifice on the cross, screams out to me saying; the battle is not yours, the battle is mine. This is simply the reason why Our Creator died, it was to cover us when we made decisions that worked against us instead of for us.

In my time away from God I figured I just needed to be independent. I couldn't trust men, I couldn't trust friends and I couldn't trust God. I figured all I would need to survive would be myself. I forgot that although I had become strong on the outside, I was still hurting deep on the inside. True inner and outer strength comes from God. The Bible talks about being strong and courageous over 116 times, but it never says to be strong and courageous all by yourself. I became so overwhelmed with my problems and situations that I stopped praying and seeking Gods presence. I thought I had it all under control. I didn't need anyone or anything. I was right in believing I didn't need the ones who abused me, but I definitely needed God, the one who could restore me.

It Does Get Better…

I was coming to terms with what I needed to change in my life and in my heart day to day. And with my mother right by my side, I began to heal. The healing started from the hurts of my past to realizing what I had to change in my present. With time, the bits and pieces of my life started falling back into place. I was alone for quite some time. I had dedicated my life to raise my daughter.

After diligently looking for work, I got a job and was able to get on my feet again. With my first check, I gave my tithes to my mother—not even realizing I was confirming a word of God to her. My mother was on her last day, of a 40 day fast. God was calling her to pastor and told her the legacy of ministry in her family would continue through her. When I got my first check, I gave my mother 10% of my gross income and told her, "this goes to a pastor," and innocently gave her the check. My mother began to cry and thank God. She knew then, God was calling her and it wasn't her emotions.

When my daughter was just shy of being 4 years old, my friend took me out to get me away from my daily routine. It was there where I met my husband, Jay.

I was at the lowest point in my life. I wasn't looking for a relationship, but when he asked me for my number, I gave it to him. We spoke about church on our first few dates, and how we needed God in our lives. We quickly introduced each other to our families and began to date. He loved my daughter instantly. He bought her gifts and made her laugh. He had no problems being around her or putting her first in our courtship. He didn't have an issue calling her his daughter without anyone asking him too. He was caring, thoughtful, was the first in his family to graduate with his Bachelor's Degree, had a great job and his own place and may I add, very tall, muscular and handsome. I could date someone like this. He understood my background and my culture.

During our courtship, I knew I needed and wanted more in my life. Jay and I had a great time for the first 6 months of our relationship, but I started to notice he had a drinking problem. He didn't drink every day, but when we went out, he didn't know how to stop drinking until he passed out. We were on shaky grounds. I wasn't use to this, nor wanted to expose my daughter to this behavior. After 6 months in our relationship, he lost his job and I saw a different side of him.

I had to make a change. God was calling me back to His presence, but I didn't know how to go back. My mother was pastoring a church already, but I wanted my own private experience. A well-known evangelist was going to be at Madison Square Garden preaching, and Jay and I decided to go. What a breath of fresh air. I was home again. The preacher was speaking right to me. I ran to get prayed for. I felt the cleansing of God and gave my heart to the Lord. I was born again. I was home.

I was changing my life completely around. I was choosing life and freedom and keeping it that way. Because I didn't want to live a life of sin, I broke up with Jay. He couldn't understand what was going on, but what he did understand was that I loved God more than anything else and I wasn't going to mess up this time. He saw my commitment and diligence, something he never seen before, and gave his heart to God as well. God delivered him from alcoholism, we began a business that changed his life through the association of men of God, men of integrity and character. A year later, we were married.

My mother married us. It was an honor for us to be married by her. We became closer than ever. We became each other's rock. She ordained me again, this time to be a Reverend and assist with pastoring her church. My mother's goal is to ordain all her children when the time is right.

I attribute my return to Christ to my mother's prayers. There's power when you have a prayer warrior in your corner who stands in the gap for you. All I needed to do then was decide what I wanted to do. Did I want to continue to be bitter and fool around? Or did I want to be healed and restored? Did I want to give another go to life? I choose another go to life. I was focused this time more than ever

We have life coaches and mentors besides God and my mother, who have guided us towards a strong marriage, good parenting, and financial independence. We're serving under my mother's ministry, "House of Prayer & Restoration, Inc."

We had a second child, which has united the family even more We've placed our daughters' in ballet, tap dance, swimming, piano, soccer, and violin classes, private school and whatever would help them grow well rounded. We're humbled to say, through God's grace we've purchased our first home and paid off our mortgage... We've purchased our cars and done well with our business and jobs. I've been constantly promoted and recognized at my day job for over achieving sales quota for over 15 years. And a personal goal of mine, I really thought was unreachable, my credit score went from 200 to an 858.

I don't say this to impress you, but to impress upon you that God's grace and mercy can get you back on track regardless of the time you've thought you've lost. To God there is not time. He is the Alpha and Omega, the First and the Last, the Beginning and the End. Revelation 22:13. God will recoup it, if you put Him first in your life, everything else will come in addition to it.

But seek first His kingdom and His Righteousness, and all these things will be given unto you as well. Matthew 6:33.

It all seemed so far away in the beginning, but I decided not to live like the bitter people I was associating with. Part of the process was letting go of the things and people who were holding me back. Some people didn't want to see me succeed and even some of those people were family and friends. They didn't want me to move on. They wanted me to stay a victim and be in the bottom of the barrel with them. Once I overcame all that pain and decided to move on and let go, I lost people in my life. But I knew my freedom and my joy was more important than hanging out with the people who only wanted to bicker and moan.

People do not determine your future. Don't let the pain of this world determine your future either. Let your pain determine your destiny in God.

There are no coincidences in God. He has a plan for you whether you believe it or not. You were meant to be here. You are not a mistake. Everything you've been through can be used as a stepping stone to achieve your dreams and goals. There is a purpose for your life. The work is finding out what is your destiny and following it regardless of the obstacles that come your way. Understand the obstacles come to give your patience and character. They don't come to destroy you but to make you a person that you are meant to be. Do not give up.

I didn't give up. I got that from my mom.

In the time I spent with my mother, I confided in her more and more. I wanted to know how she survived it all. I spoke to her about her struggles and her reply was astonishing.

"You had to forgive him."

Breaking generational curses...

You have read about two women, two generations, same situation, same cycle but with the same opportunity of be free through forgiveness. We chose to forgive. My mother forgave my father and I forgave him too. I forgave my ex-husband and she forgave him too. When we chose to forgive amazing things happened. First, we forgave by obedience then we forgave by choice, but the reality was that we chose to forgive because we learned how to love our selves more than the pain. We forgave ourselves. We understood we deserved to be happy and decided to start a new cycle of blessings in our family.

Can you truly forgive someone?

Yes, forgiveness is a choice. Yes, you can forgive yourself. But here's the thing: while we may accept these statements on the surface, we often have trouble following through on the act of forgiveness – be it forgiving ourselves or someone else.

After we forgave ourselves, we forgave the rest of the people who hurt us.

Right here started Beauty for Ashes.

CHAPTER 13

I LOVE MY DADDY…

In my process of healing I realized I needed to address the root to a lot of my issues. I had made it to the point where it was time to forgive the person who started it all and move on from the past so that I could be the woman I was meant to be.

I want to make very clear in this book that I love my dad, I honor my dad and I respect my dad even though these things happened. I am merely uncovering sin that has been hidden in many families of power for generations. **Mark 4:22 says,** "For whatever is hidden is meant to be disclosed, and whatever is concealed is meant to be brought out into the open."

It is time to stand in the gap for those families that have been suffering with this abuse and let them know there's a way out of this curse. It is possible to live a blessed life and break those generational curses over our children and children's, children.

If we do not confront the devil and keep our sin hidden, how are we going to deal with our next generation? How are we going to pass the baton of generational blessings if we keep these situations behind closed doors, keeping the curse over our future generations?

I needed to forgive him for myself and for my daughters and their children to come. I was going to break the generational cycle once and for all. I've decided to follow the commandment of forgiveness and made a choice, whether I felt it or not to forgive him. The Bible says, first commandment with a promise in Exodus 20:12, "Honor your father and mother, so that your days may be long in the land that the LORD your God is giving you." It then reinforces it in the New Testament in Matthew 15:4 and Mark 7:10 "For God said, 'Honor your father and mother' and 'Anyone who curses their father or mother (speaks disrespectfully or speak evil of them) is to be put to death.'

The Bible is merely a set of instructions for our daily living. It's a set of instructions on how to live a joyful life in the mist of this destructive world. We have nothing to lose to follow it, but so much to gain if we do.

At first, any time I told my father I forgave him for something, he didn't understand. At times I didn't understand it either. I had every right to be a rebellious, bitter and broken woman but, was that who I wanted to be forever?

Though there is never really any excuse for abuse I took the time to understand where my father come from. He was never taught the love of a parent and unfortunately, he never took out the time to learn or had the correct mentors to teach him to do so. I would end that in my family. My children would be loved and valued by both their parents. My husband and I make sure of it.

A narcissistic person doesn't have the ability to take responsibility for his action or wants to for that matter. Although I confronted my father many times and didn't get the response I was always seeking, I didn't change my plans of forgiving him. I understood, I had to let go and move on.

As time has passed, I've reached out to my father to begin a healthier relationship. I've decided to follow the commandment of forgiveness and made a choice.

One way to Forgive is to change your mind set about forgiveness...

Forgiveness is a privilege given by God to free our souls and free up space in our minds for creativity to fulfill all the gifts God has given you. We were endowed with the seeds of greatness. You were designed for accomplishments. Lack of forgiveness ties you down to bitterness. Your whole life and decisions are based on the bitterness you feel. How are you going to become who you were created to be if you're not making decisions with a clear mind?

Forgiveness gives you clarity. It gives you peace. And after years of walking on egg shells in my own house, I deserved some peace and I was not going to let it slip from my fingers.

To forgive doesn't mean:

- Forcing yourself to forget the past
- Denying what was done to you
- Letting time erase what happened
- Staying away from your abuser or running back to your abuser
- Ignoring what happened and being indifferent to the people who hurt you
- Excusing the abuser
- Saying 'I forgive you' just to say it without any intentions of actually forgiving

Forgiveness is:

- For me
- Canceling the debt
- Releasing the person who hurt you and releasing yourself
- Freeing the person who hurt you and freeing yourself
- Having compassion

- Making the decision to forgive as an act of free will.
- Being like Christ
- Understanding that God forgave us first. John 3:16.
- Being merciful – To be merciful brings us mercy Matthew 5:7, "Blessed are the merciful for they shall obtain mercy."
- If you want forgiveness, give forgiveness, Matthew 7:12 – "therefore, whatever you want men to do to you, do also to them"

Forgiveness Produces Freedom & Peace - John 8:36 – "So if the Son sets you free, you will be free indeed" God just doesn't want us to be free but to be free indeed.

Now I'm walking in freedom. Now I am free.

Being thankful helps you to keep walking in forgiveness.

BEING THANKFUL Helps you to Forgive

I thank my father for giving me life. I thank him for putting us in church where I learned my foundation in God and had my first encounter with Him. I thank my father because through everything I went through, I became a leader. I learned how to be an event planner, speak in public, analyze the Bible, counsel, serve, how to give selflessly, work hard and so much more.

My father taught me commitment and I thank him for that. I remember one of the only times my mom let me go outside to play, I broke my wrist. My sister and I were playing in the swings and I fell off. My sister quickly took me and ran to the house with me to tell my mom I needed to go to the hospital.

While in the hospital, I woke up in the middle of the anesthesia and saw my dad and mom over me watching the doctors operate on my arm. I saw my dad in a suit ready to go to church because he never missed church. Rain or 10 feet of snow, he was at church. I remember him brushing my hair with his hand and telling me everything was going to be okay. That was enough for me to know he loved me. We went to church well or sick. Thank God all the time we went to church sick, we came back home healed. Thank God for His mercy.

One main reason why my mother got healed from anxiety and depression was because she was thankful throughout her circumstances. She learned to thank God despite the circumstances.

Once I began forgiving for everything that happened to me, I found myself ready to forgive the man I thought I would share a life with forever. Despite it all, though it took time, I came to the place where I could forgive my ex-husband. I'm thankful for the time we shared together. You took my mind off my loneliness for a while and without you I wouldn't have my eldest. You were a part of my journey to becoming the woman I am today and I thank you for that.

CHAPTER 14

WHAT MAKES YOU MISERABLE TODAY, YOU WILL THANK GOD FOR TOMORROW…

Don't put too much energy in a place you are about to leave.

My mother and I are no longer surviving. We're thriving; living the best days of our lives. We're finally free and free indeed. We've decided to be better and not bitter.

We needed to go through those trials and tribulations to become the women of strength God had created us to be and to know how to navigate through the storms of our children's lives and others lives. He gave us the tools necessary to bring freedom and victory to those around us. God gave us the vision and provided the provision.

We've become the lighthouse and many ships have sailed to our light to find peace and restoration through Jesus Christ. We counsel men and women who have gone through or are going through our same situation. We have clarity on seeing the purpose of why we went through those years of torment and thank God today, for the misery we went through yesterday.

Whatever you are going through today is to make you into the person you need to be tomorrow. Embrace the journey of growth, of pain, of struggle, and development to become the person God has destined you to be. Understand that ***It's the blind spots that give you focus.*** You're not supposed to know everything, but you are supposed to hang on to your Creator through the process.

We know without a shadow of a doubt that part of our destiny is helping people get out of their abusive relationships; empowering those with low self-esteem and educating the emotionally sick on inner healing and restoration. We have understood the bigger the struggle, the bigger the blessing.

There is Purpose in Your Pain

We are living the best days of our lives because we understood we needed to forgive.

We Moved on Because We Forgave

If more people would embrace forgiveness, we would have more peace in this world.

Forgiveness Heals

Forgiveness healed my mother from so many diseases. She was suffering with manic depression and extreme anxiety. As I mentioned before, she was told she needed medication, or she would go crazy. She looked at the prescription, wrinkled it up and said out loud, "I am healed in the name of Jesus." There's power in the words that come out of your mouth. Proverbs 18:21 (NIV) says, 21." The tongue has the power of life and death, and those who love it will eat its fruit." You're either bless or curse with the words that come out of your mouth. My mother's confessions healed her through her belief that she was already healed by God. Her confidence in God took her to levels of healing and restoration beyond her understanding.

A few months after, she got severe asthma out of nowhere. She never had experienced any issues with her breathing. She was 44 years old and physically healthy when her divorce was final. I remember sleeping beside her and being annoyed all night because of her constant cough. She went to the doctors and sporadically took the medication but had a strong confidence in God that she would be healed. I saw her faith surpass her fears and struggles.

One random Sunday at Thessalonica Church, as the pastor, Rev. David Serrano was preaching, she felt a strong conviction that her healing was near. She was at the right place at the right time. The pastor prayed for her, and suddenly all cough was gone. Her chest was cleared, and the asthma never came back. I saw it with my own eyes. All this because she chose to forgive.

Years later the doctor diagnosed her with breast cancer. My mother told the doctor right there and then, "I don't accept those words, I am healed in the name of Jesus." I was panicking and she was calming me down. She had a pending trip to preach in Puerto Rico and decided to go against the doctors wishes. When she returned, she knew for sure she was healed. I was so nervous when she went back to the doctors for another biopsy. The results came back, free and clear. NO CANCER. I cried so much. I even made a video on the whole process. God is real.

She got healed of bursitis in her right shoulder. Doctors told her the only way she will move forward from the shoulder pain was getting surgery. She said no, "I'm healed in the name of Jesus," and surely enough, she was. She never owned the pain nor the sickness. She never called it hers. She would say things like "that's not my sickness." I am healed in the name of Jesus. Words are truly powerful. Be careful what you call yours.

I myself have been healed from depression and anxiety. I've been healed of bursitis on my right arm and a close call of breast cancer. All because my mother taught me not to own what the doctors say, and above all believe and have faith in the Word of God.

Do Not Own Something that Wasn't Meant to be Yours

We chose to be FREE

If it's Still Living in Your Heart, it's Still Living in Your Mind

A few years after my mother began to pastor, the church was flourishing, and my brothers and I were all working with her to grow the church and serve the community. I saw the way my mother interacted with my father. We could have Thanksgiving together and Christmas together. I saw first-hand her forgiveness. I saw my older brother and the rest of my family forgive him. Her behavior united the family once again.

I remember my mother visiting my father in the hospital and telling him she forgave him. She forgave the women my father left with long before she came back crying to my mother for forgiveness. There was no bitterness, no hatred, no revenge in her heart but true forgiveness. It wasn't in her head nor in her mind.

How do you know when you forgave? When you can Pray for those that hurt you.

The Key to Restoration and Inner Healing is Forgiveness

Some people embrace bitterness so strong that they become one with it. It's almost like they are married to bitterness and anger. They feel like they are cheating on bitterness if they entertain forgiveness. They don't understand that letting go; divorcing forgiveness, is what is going to make them free. It's what is going to allow them to live a life of abundance and freedom. Choose to be obedient and follow the commandment of forgiveness. The Bible talks about God wanting obedience more than sacrifice. Proverbs 21:3 (NIV) says, [3] "To do what is right and just is more acceptable to the Lord than sacrifice." Choose forgiveness. Your life will never be the same again.

If you never well on the inside, you will never be the person God has created you to be.

The second portion of John 10:10 talks about the abundance of life. Abundance means getting more and more. Your life is getting better and better. Because the devil couldn't kill us and we prevailed, our lives are increasingly getting better and better. From the people that surround us to our prosperity with our health, emotions, and finances; it's just getting better.

My mother's abundance of love and forgiveness to my father spilled over to all of us. It was a super natural love we have seen from her. A love when you don't want to or when you don't feel it. Love is not a feeling. Love is action. My mother knew that if she showed the love of God to my father by her actions even if she didn't feel it, the love of God would overwhelm us, and true inner healing would be a consequence of those actions.

Guard Your Heart

It's very important to understand that forgiveness does not necessarily mean that you must begin a relationship or become involved with your abuser. Although my father did return to my mother and wanted to have a relationship with her, she understood that was not the will of God for her. She had moved on from that period of her life. They have a platonic relationship for the sake of the children and grandchildren, and they do talk occasionally but are not together.

It is beautiful that all of us have forgiven my father in many ways. We all have our story and have lived different lives and have had different challenges because of the events that I've discussed, but at the end of the day because of my mother's love and forgiveness, we've all been able to find our way towards true healing.

God removed everyone who hated on my mother; everyone who hurt my mother, everyone who desired her pain, God exalted her right in front of them.

My mother, not too long ago was able to own a home. A complete miracle of God. Being a real estate agent, I never saw someone own a home without a job or a W2. But somehow, God made it happen. All her children are happily married; healthy, professionals, have homes and are prosperous. Everything God has put in her hands has prospered. The church she pastors gives to everyone in need. Pastors and ministers have run to our church to be financially and spiritually blessed. She has always given and never borrowed. Because of her obedience; her children, grandchildren, great grandchildren and generations to come are blessed.

People are People

People are people and they will make their own choices—even in the church. Understand that just like college is a place to go study, not everyone does. Like the gym is a place everyone gets in shape, not everyone does. A relationship with our creator surpasses all the nonsense that happens in churches. None of what I experienced changes the reality of who God is. It does not change the Word of God.

So, what is it to PREVAILING…?

- It's to win every day by controlling your thoughts
- It's to turn your pain into power
- It's to help someone else when you need help
- It's to forgive even though it doesn't make sense
- It's to understand pain is temporary

- It's to understand life is a journey of struggles that bring you closer to your destiny as you overcome them
- It's prevailing to reach to the next level
- It's to get use to fighting, understanding the next fight will begin when the first fight is over.
- It's to be thankful
- It's to succeed against all odds
- It's knowing the truth
- It's knowing you are more than a conqueror
- It's knowing you're not alone in your fight
- It's knowing God is in the process with you and He has already Prevailed for you
- It's knowing the battle has already been won
- It's knowing the battle is not yours, it's Gods.

As I finish this book, I am so grateful to have a mother that has shown me how to prevail through the storms in my life. She's taught me that overcoming through struggles is a part of life. We are either prevailing through a struggle, prevailing out of a struggle or prevailing into a struggle. Prevailing is ongoing. I'm so glad I have a mother whose strength and dedication to God allowed me to overcome my own.

The goal of writing this book was to demonstrate the power of reconciliation. Now that you know my mother's story and my story, I can say that there is no better way to live this life through the freedom of reconciliation. Reconciliation with yourself, with others and with God through forgiveness.

Maybe at this moment you are in the same situation that my mother or myself were. I want to invite you to start with the first step of healing, which is to recognize the need to live a life of reconciliation. After you have recognized the need, I encourage you to invite Jesus Christ into your heart. He will give you the strength and true love that we all seek. Romans 10:9 NIV- "If you declare with your mouth, "Jesus is Lord," and believe in your heart that God raised him from the dead, you will be saved." Second, I invite you to go to a Bible teaching church. Thirdly, you contact me, and we can grow together in this process of reconciliation and freedom.

God Bless You all and let's live the best life Our Creator Has intended us to live before the foundations of this world!

Instagram - @prevailthebook

Facebook – Author- Jinary Cotto

Email - Jinary@optonline.net